THE
WORKING
BEDLINGTON

Acknowledgements

My grateful thanks to everyone who willingly and kindly co-operated in supplying photographic material for this book, namely Ian Johnson, Steven Robinson, David Murray, D. P. Glover, Jackie Ison, Jim Davies, Caroline Pindred, Philip Booker, R. F. Penrose, P. Hood and Laurie Fergusson. Also my very special thanks to George Newcombe for sharing his wealth of knowledge on the Bedlington Terrier.

Contents

This book is dedicated to my wife for being so patient and to 'Old Blue', a dear friend who fell ill while the book was being completed.

Dickson Price Publishers Ltd.
Hawthorn House
Bowdell Lane
Brookland
Romney Marsh
Kent TN29 9RW

First published 1990
© John Robert Glover

British Library Cataloguing in Publication Data

Glover, John Robert
  The working Bedlington.
  1. Bedlington terriers
  I. Title
  636.7'55

ISBN 0–85380–112–6

Set by R. H. Services, Welwyn, Hertfordshire
Printed and bound by Biddles Ltd, Guildford and King's Lynn.

THE
WORKING
BEDLINGTON

JOHN ROBERT GLOVER

DICKSON PRICE

Introduction

It is often said, 'One man's meat is another man's poison', and certainly this appears to be true judging by the differences of opinion among Bedlington terrier enthusiasts. Perhaps I'd better explain. At present two types of Bedlington terrier exist – a show-type and a working-type, the former being the more familiar. It is, however, the working-type with which this book is concerned and I hope that these pages will prove a useful guide to the true situation regarding what it has now become fashionable to term a 'working-type Bedlington terrier'.

The original Bedlington terrier was a great little dog, famed for it's character and bottomless, blind courage. Good enough to be termed an all-round working terrier and equally at home staying to and bolting a tough northern fox, as it was slaying farmyard rats, being the companion and guard of the family and providing the odd family dinner, be it a rabbit or an unwary pheasant.

To fulfil these roles therefore, the dog had to conform to the basic requisites of a working terrier, which cannot sadly be said in all truthfulness of the modern-day, show-type Bedlington. Even the novice working-terrier person is aware, after a casual glance, that the show dog has faults as a working terrier. Especially noticeable in the show-type Bedlington are it's soft, poor coat, pale colouration, it's large height at withers, small jaws and teeth, short roached back and it's totally un-terrierish disposition.

It is my sincere hope that these pages may instil interest, indeed confidence, in all those who want to see a resurgence in the true working-type of Bedlington – which was, without doubt a superb all-round terrier. It was the mid-nineteen fifties that brought about a change in fashion and ultimately, type. A newer, elegant, more poodle-type of Bedlington was becoming increasingly more popular as a show bench winner. People were faced with a simple choice, to win, to breed this new type, or not to win, discontinue showing seriously and keep the working-type Bedlington terrier.

What happened is history, for many people opted for the former and, naturally, the Bedlington like so many of the other terrier breeds systematically suffered. Happily, thanks to the efforts of a small number of enthusiasts the true Bedlington has survived.

—1—

What is a Working Bedlington?

I T WAS DURING the 1970s when the first stirrings of a revival of interest in the Bedlington terrier as a working dog began to emerge. Several factors influenced this, including fashion, press coverage and the 'boomtime' that was about to begin with the lurcher. Of course, lurcher-type dogs had always been popular with the poverty-stricken working classes, where scarce money and large families in many cases necessitated that if a dog were to be kept at all, 'he must earn his corn'. Lurchers, crossbred as they are, were crossed often with the collie to the greyhound for the larger version, and as often as not, between the Bedlington terrier and the whippet in the smaller rabbit-snatching variety.

The cross Bedlington/whippet or occasionally greyhound, certainly produced an attractive lurcher and with the advent of the lurcher shows, Bedlington crosses started to win well, at least in the under 23 inch classes. At a time when it became very 'hip' to own a lurcher, especially an attractive one, the Bedlington cross, and ultimately the pure-bred working Bedlington, came once again into public view and more and more Bedlingtons of all types and sizes started turning up at the game fairs and country shows. Those folks who have attended the Northern and East Midland terrier and lurcher shows will, I am sure, be familiar with John Piggin (the Newark Rat Catcher) and his wife Sheila, who have supported and attended many of these shows in these areas. In actual fact, many of the working-type dogs in the Midlands contain the bloodlines of one of his two most popular stud dogs to date, both liver in colour; these are and were the late 'Jasper of Kentene' and 'Floyd of Eakring'.

Not only did the lurcher and terrier shows influence interest in the Bedlington as a working terrier, the field sports press also

9

Three Bedlingtons checking earths.

carried features and the occasional letters on the dogs, and it may have seemed positive action was at last taking shape, especially with the formation of the Working Bedlington Terrier Club and latterly the Working-type Bedlington Terrier Association. On the face of it then, it appeared that people were beginning to get interested, indeed involved in keeping alive the working-type Bedlington. On reflection perhaps the term working-type was one of the loosest descriptions ever given, for it meant anyone who owned a Bedlington, be it working strain or show strain that did some work, either a little ratting or rabbiting, stated that the dog was a 'working-type Bedlington'.

To set the record perfectly straight from the beginning, there are at present (though this hopefully will change in the future), only two lines of real working Bedlingtons. These are the Gutchcommon and Rillington lines, working-bred, but initially from *old type* show stock, terriers which justifiably merited being termed work or show. There is no doubt in my mind that the same cannot be said of today's counterparts. Today's Gutchcommon and Rillington-bred dogs are in a different world to those show-bred dogs from other lines that often masquerade as working-type dogs at working-terrier shows, and certainly I cannot think of a show-bred Bedlington that could compare with a Gutchcommon dog coat-wise. In fact, Mrs Margaret Williamson, who kept the Gutchcommon line, laboured on this point specifically, and indeed the Gutchcommons had superb coats.

However, Mrs Williamson's ideas of keeping alive the old type of Bedlington were very different from those of George Newcombe of Rillington, near Malton, in North Yorkshire. George, whose appropriately named Rillington Bedlingtons are generally accepted as the 'other strain' in working-Bedlington parlance, believed the old type of dog could not be maintained and kept alive, purely within the confines of the breed, and set about creating the old-fashioned type of Bedlington terrier by way of introducing both pedigree lakeland and un-registered fell terrier blood. As one may imagine, this met with quite some controversy, especially with those people who were concerned specifically with keeping Kennel Club Registration at all costs.

Although holding conflicting viewpoints, the two major pioneers of the working-type Bedlington of recent years, Mrs Williamson and George Newcombe, were united by one common dislike, namely the poodle likeness so admired and adored by the show fanciers. With the formation of the first working club, The Working Bedlington Terrier Club, Mrs Williamson's Gutchcommon dogs

11

did become very popular, indeed the problem was, how to continue breeding the type without breeding any closer. (The strain was already inbred enough as it was, as a glance at some GC pedigrees will prove.)

George silenced his critics with his early attempts at out-crossing and in actual fact succeeded in his first generation Bedlington/lakeland hybrids, to reproduce very closely dogs that resembled the very early Bedlingtons. To have some idea what those early dogs of the Rothbury Forest looked like, we must take a trip back in time to the very beginning of Bedlington history.

—2—

History

WITH MOST BREEDS of dog, accurate history and origins can be very sketchy indeed, and some of the theories put forward about the Bedlington are certainly inaccurate, but amusing none the less.

A real peach is the continental gypsy theory, which has it that these wandering tribes required a coursing dog and created the early Bedlington, which they certainly did not. An amalgamation of greyhound, whippet, otterhound and Dandie Dinmont are supposed to have gone into the making of this gypsy Bedlington. It is of course quite possible that the early Bedlingtons could have been kept by border gypsies, though certainly not as their coursing dogs and not of their creation. Another colourful and equally misleading theory is that miners created them for going down the mines and killing rats, and although certainly I'd agree that any rat unlucky enough to cross paths with a Bedlington down a mine would undoubtedly find the situation pretty grim, I do not accept that the Bedlington was created for this reason alone.

The Dandie Dinmont terrier though did play a part, and was a first cousin, both breeds being descended from a common ancestor. Before anyone voices the opinion that the Bedlington and the Dandie Dinmont bear no resemblance to each other, they would do well to remember that the modern Dandie is as different from it's early ancestors as is the show-type Bedlington. It is my belief that far from the Bedlington terrier being a gypsy dog, it was developed within a locality by certain sportsmen in the early 1800s. In point of fact, the early Dandie and Bedlington were developed very close to each other. One interesting fact is that the town of Bedlington is approximately eighteen miles away from this location, which is Rothbury in the Coquet Valley. Surely a more

13

A nineteenth century Bedlington.

A fine looking working Bedlington of today.

appropriate name for the Bedlington terrier, certainly a more accurate one geographically, would have been the Rothbury terrier. 'Redmarshall' in his book *The Bedlington Terrier History and Origin* (published by Dickson Price Publishers Ltd.) takes this a step further and suggests not only Rothbury as a more accurate name, but also Framlington, Longhorseley or any of the other villages from which the Bedlington's ancestors came.

Two owners of these early dogs came from the tiny hamlet of Holystone, four and a half miles away from Rothbury, and from other sources we see that many of these early dogs were very closely in-bred, brother to sister being the most favoured mating. It is interesting to note that the hamlet of Holystone was the home of James Allan, who died in 1810, owner of the ancestors of what later became the Dandie Dinmont. One of these was known as Piper Allan because of his love of playing the bagpipes. Redmarshall certainly believed, as I do, that the early ancestors of both the Dandie and the Bedlington were one and the same. So convinced was Redmarshall of this, that he observed that the ancestors of the Bedlington were in fact the same as of Piper Allan's dogs, which were the dogs reputed to be the ancestors of the Dandie Dinmont.

It is also worthy of note that reputedly the ancestors of the terrier now known as the border were also Piper Allan's dogs. According to Redmarshall he believed a dog called Old Peacham belonging to Donkin of Flotterton (four miles from Holystone) was of Piper Allan's strain and it was mated to Evan's Vixen and Turnbull's Venom, both of whom lived at Holystone. Both of these matings appear in the pedigree of Pheobe mother of Piper, the first Bedlington. For the next 50 years the Bedlington was a breed developed purely as a working terrier. In comparing the present-day Bedlington with it's ancestors one need go no further than a description of the parents of Piper, that first Bedlington by name. His sire, Old Piper, was a slender dog of approximately 15 inches in height, weighing 15 pounds, he was a liver-coloured animal with a coat of woolly-hard lint, and his large full drop ears with their feathered tips completed his physical appearance.

Likewise, Pheobe (Piper's dam) stood 13 inches high, weighed 14 pounds, was black/blue in colour and had the characteristic light silky top-knot on her head. Where does one find dogs of this ilk nowadays? Dogs that are not too frail to operate in the traditional Bedlington manner – closing on their quarry, reluctant to give ground at any cost and displaying the hallmark of a true Bedlington's nature, blind courage – something those early dogs were famed for.

It is well over 200 years ago that Thomas Gainsborough's third Duke of Buccleuch was painted. In the portrait, the duke is pictured with his arm around a much-loved pet; the dog in question might well be a Dandie Dinmont. Whatever it was, the Buccleuch's were associated with the Bedlington/Dandie type or most certainly its forbears (the Dandie is generally associated with the Buccleuch's).

It is generally recognised that the Bedlington, the Dandie Dinmont and the border terrier are all blood relatives. It is established that a degree of cross breeding went on within these three breeds. We have already established a link via the three through Piper Allen's dogs, and if we needed another pointer to this theory, we need look no further than one of the border terrier's original names – the Coquetdale terrier. Rothbury is in the Coquet Valley of Northumberland, an area where the ancestors of the early Bedlington's lived. So it is proved that prior to registration when these three breeds were developed purely for their ability at vermin destruction, crossing was not only accepted it was deemed necessary.

After those first 50 years and the start of its show career, the Bedlington still maintained the ability to work and more importantly perhaps still displayed the legendary Bedlington courage. According to George Newcombe, even the post-war dogs could be relied upon to be sound in this respect, even if the breed had by now drifted towards being too big. In fact, George's early dogs were bred from dogs of this period, including the famous Rillington Rinty, a dog George rates as his hardest ever, and he has often told me of the dog's fearless uncompromising nature. Apparently Rinty entered a fox earth with only two things in his mind – either to find and kill his fox as soon as he could, or alternatively to simply draw Charlie. An interesting fact is that many people since the 1950s, mostly non dog owners, ask if show-type Bedlingtons are poodles or poodle crosses; just occasionally one hears other suppositions a little more complimentary, like – Is it a whippet?, or It's like a curly-coated bull terrier. Incidentally both the whippet and the Staffordshire bull terrier are rumoured also to be in the Bedlington's early ancestry, but neither rumour bears scrutiny and neither is correct.

Speaking of Staffordshire bull terriers, in more recent times Stafford cross Bedlington matings have taken place, though it should be pointed out, not in the production of a Bedlington-type dog; more I fancy as a novelty-cross, or as an attempt to produce a hard-bitten working terrier. The theory that the bull breed was in

16

the early Bedlington's make-up is easy to understand and just as easy to dispel, as the following short tale will reveal. In the early part of the nineteenth century, a colony of Staffordshire nailmakers is reputed to have moved to Northumberland and it is presumed they took their dogs with them. It is generally accepted that the dogs would be of a fighting breed, bull, or bull and terrier and according to the theory these dogs were crossed with the local terrier to produce the Bedlington, pretty flimsy evidence I'd say, especially when one considers that Bedlington-type terriers were not only being bred at that time relatively pure but were also being bred very closely (they certainly would not have needed an outcross).

Another consideration to be observed was that the Bedlington at that time was as game an animal as could ever be found and certainly would not have needed any bull terrier blood to 'pep it up'. Quite the reverse was the truth of the matter, the Bedlington was generally acknowledged as good foundation stock and clearly played a part in the creation later on of the patterdale, and eventually the lakeland terrier.

Perhaps it is expedient to deviate slightly at this stage and define what I mean by patterdale terrier. The original patterdale was not only different physically to the smooth-coated black and red terriers so very popular at today's working-terrier shows, it was also of a very different temperament. More often than not it was blue or brown in colour, and also in some cases showed very clearly it's Bedlington ancestry. The story of Tommy Dobson using a Bedlington as an outcross to his fell terrier, to give the dogs guts, is by now a pretty famous one.

Those Bedlingtons of a bygone age were real all-rounders, they went to ground on foxes in an area where fox killing was essential work rather than sport, they tackled the now illegal pastime of badger digging, worked at rats, and helped provide for the poacher's family. How anybody who really cared for the charm of these little dogs could ruin their nature just for the sake of beauty evades me.

This book explores the ways in which the Bedlington can continue as a working terrier and also the opposing theories held by the late Mrs Margaret Williamson who had kept and bred her own pure strain for at least 60 years and those held by George Newcombe who outcrosses to other breeds.

—3—

Saving the Real Bedlington

I N THE EARLY 1980s the very thought of crossing one's Bedlington with another breed of terrier in a bid to produce a better working dog would have been greeted by some people with gasps of horror. Mrs Margaret Williamson, a great champion for the cause of the real Bedlington, and George Newcombe, equally as staunch a supporter had a great deal of disagreement regarding this idea. Mrs Williamson, whilst in utmost agreement that a breeding programme be set up to revive the breed, was of the opinion the breed could be saved by pairing the very best working-type dogs together. Although in principal this seemed the right approach, in practice there was a problem in that some working-type dogs were already very closely inbred.

Whether or not this degree of inbreeding had already had a detrimental effect upon the lines in question is very much a matter of personal opinion, but certainly the opinions available were stacked against the supporter of the pure-bred dog. It is my opinion that certain dogs although very inbred were still sound, though some, more often bitches, were on the narrow dividing line between sound and being either too frail or small to work underground to a fox. That dividing line is a very tiny one, believe me. Apart from further inbreeding, which had gone just about as far as it could do, there was only one alternative using pure-bred dogs, namely modern show-stock – some alternative!

It is interesting to speculate at this stage why some people found this acceptable, yet were vehemently against outcrossing to other suitable breeds at all costs, these very same people being those who claimed to be trying to revive the working-type Bedlington.

Perhaps they conveniently dismissed outcrossing simply because it does away with their beloved Kennel Club Registration and,

18

despite decrying the show-dogs in public, will privately mate their registered working bitch to a show-type animal. I really do wonder if some use their dogs for working at all; saying their dogs work rats and rabbits is a very convenient way of justifying their dogs as working Bedlingtons and can also be very hard to disprove. Let me point out at this stage, that ratting is not only great fun, but that a good ratting dog, especially one that is going to be expected to kill a number of rats in one session needs to be a particularly valiant and game dog.

I now give a condensed version of the main points you should be breeding for in the standard below.

> A lightly built but muscular dog, 15 inches in height with a long, well-proportioned body.
> Back slightly arched, long and flexible, shoulders flat.
> Chest and front narrow with a long, strong neck and head – combining both powerful jaws with big teeth.
> Coat hard, wiry outer coat, and dense.
> Colours black/blue, dark-liver or any of these two combined with tan.

My conclusion is that today's show-bred dogs are not game enough to be used in a breeding programme whose purpose is the production of working-type Bedlingtons. The only practical choice for the owners of pure-bred working-type Bedlingtons who wish their dogs to remain that way is to go for more inbreeding, which is not to be recommended, although it is a more viable and sensible proposition than the alternative of using show-type dogs.

The lakeland outcross
When that inimitable character George Newcombe of Rillington in North Yorkshire came up with the brainwave of crossing his Rillington-bred Bedlingtons with his lakeland terriers, Mrs Williamson, the owner of the Gutchcommon prefix could not endorse his suggestion, and this probably led to George Newcombe deciding to leave his post as chairman of the Working Bedlington Terrier Club. It has taken from those early days to the present time for his idea to really appeal to a wide range of people, and in fact many people now voice the opinion that they would like to own an outcrossed dog, particularly novices, as they believe it will be a more reliable and terrier-like animal than is normally the case with some pure-bred Bedlingtons, the type that George Newcombe so often refers to as pseudo-Bedlingtons.

George, a perfectionist to the core, is very, very careful

A lakeland/Bedlington.

A lakeland terrier.

surrounding his choice of a lakeland as an outcross, to say the least, preferring to use his own Rillington lakelands rather than a suspect dog and he would never consider using a terrier that he believes has either Welsh, or wire fox-terrier breeding. George once said to me, 'it's as hard to find a real lakeland nowadays as it is to find a good Bedlington'.

A criticism one so often hears of cross-breeding is that the dogs are no longer pedigree. Treat this kind of statement with the contempt it deserves, for I do not know anyone who actively outcrosses that does not give authentic written pedigrees with the dogs they eventually breed, pedigrees which are as every bit as accurate, I might add, as for any dog registered with the Kennel Club.

The dachshund outcross

Dave Parsons from Kent tried an experimental mating by using a miniature wire-haired dachshund to a Bedlington-type bitch, but I gather he hit something of a snag trying to get a bitch bred from such a union, mated back to a Bedlington dog. Bedlingtons and wire-haired dachshunds share an ancestor, albeit a distant one, through the Dandie Dinmont, that was purported to have been used in the wire-haired dachshund's early creation, I don't really feel justified in commenting on such an outcross, simply because I only ever saw one photograph of the bitch. However, I do have a gut-feeling that if a Rothbury Forest or improved Dandie-type terrier were the hoped-for outcome, a better outcross (and I admit I am biased here) could be found in the form of the Irish Glen of Imaal terrier.

The Glen of Imaal outcross

Unlike either the lakeland or perhaps the dachshund, the Glen of Imaal is not a related breed and hails from Ireland, more specifically the County of Wicklow. The Glen of Imaal terrier has no breeding in common with either the Bedlington terrier or Dandie Dinmont. They are however, uncannily reminiscent of the old Dandie Dinmont, and at a sidelong glance are easily confused with them. The biggest difference between the two is their weights, and although the early Dandies were lighter than is normal today for the breed, even so the modern Dandie is still lighter in weight than the Glen of Imaal. Early Dandie Dinmonts were 16–18 lb, which is half the normal weight of a Glen of Imaal terrier.

I think most people know what a lakeland terrier looks like, although George Newcombe might say most do not know what a 'real' one looks like; however, mention a Glen of Imaal to a lot of people and they have never even heard of one let alone know what one looks like. The dog comes in two basic colours – wheaton and blue, although blue and tans exist, known by their owners sometimes as blue wheatons.

Despite the dogs coming in two different colours, all were bred as working terriers, and let me stress that in those early days in Ireland it's work demanded a very game terrier. Badger work was without doubt one of it's main functions, and the dog was also asked, in common with it's close cousins, the Kerry Blue, soft-coated wheaton and red Irish terrier to give account of itself in the barbaric past time of dog-fighting. According to sketchy history this was not conducted in a pit as with the bull-type fighting dogs used in mainland Britain, rather the spectacle took place in an open space in some secluded valley, with no rules, except possibly that only one animal walked away.

Not all of the Glen of Imaal's work was as barbaric however, as it was employed by some as a steady herding dog, and it is true that the Glen of Imaal does display a unique temperament – quite unlike the sharp yappy nature of some of the smaller hunt terriers. It's nature is more intelligent and steady, qualities it would have needed for herding. It's more usual role was as a general-purpose vermin-dog above ground and if it needed a motto it would probably be 'if it smells right, it is right'. The Irish have always had different laws from the English concerning working dogs and the example of this is the tests they used until 1966 for working terriers.

They had two tests for their underground terriers which were the Great Test, or Teastas Misneach for heavy dogs, and the Minor Test, or Teastas Beag for smaller and sounding terriers. Up to 1966 in Ireland a Glen of Imaal had to earn 16 points in show competition before it could be called Bench Champion; to gain the title of full champion, the animal would need to go on to gain either of the two test certificates. The Teastas Beag was principally an above-ground test and the dogs were tested on rat and rabbit. This basically involved releasing a rabbit in a field and when the animal had made good it's escape the terrier was released, the judges then awarding points or marks rather in today's sheepdog trial manner, for performance, scenting, ability, pursuit, style and tracking.

A variation of this trial was a water test, held either on a stream, river or canal; in this case the dog would be tested on rat. A pipe or chute fixed to a stand was built and projected over the water. The unfortunate rodent was secured in the pipe and then released into the water via the chute. The terrier was expected to enter the water and hunt the rat, either in the water or on the opposite bank. For maximum points the dog was expected to make a kill, however the actual hunt was very important in the awarding of points and the dog did not have to kill to gain the coveted Teastas Beag.

The Great Test, or Teastas Misneach was a totally different kettle of fish. Here the heavy dogs had to draw the, now thankfully illegal, quarry, badger from a typical shore (as the false sette was termed) which had a total length of 40 feet, and was approximately two feet below ground. A badger was released at the mouth of the shore and encouraged into it. After an allotted time and if he did not hit on a trap-door within the shore, a sounder (a baying terrier) was sent in to encourage the badger to do so. A special trap-door official allowed the badger through but not the baying terrier, this was stopped from following the badger through by using the cover at the trap-door.

Everything was now ready for the heavy dog to be entered. The dog was then taken to the entrance of the shore and released. The officials of the test now began their work. Basically these officials were a man with a shovel at the shore's mouth – his job was to make sure that no earth fell into the shore entrance and it remained at it's approximate standard size (eleven inches square). Number two official was the time keeper, and he checked the time it took for the terrier to engage the badger (this was verified by holding the trap-door partially open). When the dog entered the den the trap-door was then removed totally allowing the dog to try to extract the badger if at all possible. A third official, a judge, whose job was to record the times for each dog tried, also had to record points gained or lost as the case might have been. Three other men covered the whole process of the trial, mostly lying belly-down over the shore, all the time listening for any noise below ground; their jobs were probably the most crucial ones in the trial for if any of these men heard a noise, a bark, a growl, or a yelp, he held his hand up, the trial was then deemed over and the dog was disqualified as the heavy dogs were required to work completely mute.

Other officials included a trophy keeper who recorded various winner's points, and badger keepers who kept the unfortunate animals in special cages and were responsible for retiring the badgers and for supplying their replacements.

To gain the Teastas Misneach, the dog had to engage the badger in under a minute from the time he was released from the shore entrance; failure to do so resulted in it's disqualification. On engaging the badger, the dog was then allowed six minutes to draw it from the shore without any sound, be it growl, murmer or bark. The dog that achieved this would gain maximum points, but should two dogs on the day both gain maximum points the winner was decided on time discrepancy, simply the fastest dog won on the day.

It is worthy of note that after these trials, each badger was changed and a fresh one brought in, a vet examined the badger after it's time in the shore, and it was also said that after each trial day was complete all badgers were returned to their natural sette.

In defining the heavy dogs, they were: Glen of Imaals, Kerry blues, soft-coated wheaton terriers, and red Irish terriers. All these breeds needed, up to 1966, the Great Test certificates before gaining the title of full champion in Ireland.

Another variation of the last trial existed, this was called the Sounders Trial and as it's name suggests, was devised for a baying dog. The trial as such was very similar to the one just described, only the shore entrance was nine inches square rather than the eleven inches used for the heavy dogs. Similarly the dog also had a minute with which to close with the badger and as in the previous trial, failure to do so meant instant disqualification. Upon closing with the badger the bayer was, as it's description suggests, required to bark it's head off. A dog that attacked or locked upon it's badger was disqualified if it did so for more than one of the six minutes that it was required to sound. If the dog was locked on to the badger when the shore was opened the dog was also disqualified.

Thankfully, all these trials were abandoned in 1966 in Ireland and are now illegal. These accounts have been given purely as they are of historical value and the reader should be under no illusion regarding this. Badger work, either digging, or as the trials were baiting, is strictly illegal and in no way should the reader believe otherwise. In England prior to 1966 such trials would have been illegal anyway and severely dealt with.

After such a lengthy account of the Glen of Imaal's barbaric past, it is nice to be able to say that the smaller type of Glen of Imaal, weighing approximately 24 pounds, found great favour with sportsmen who partook in legitimate terrier work. Jack Chisnell formerly of Market Harborough, I believe, had a bitch who had seen action below ground with fox and accounts of small Glens who work activly to fox are too numerous to mention. The middle and large heavyweight Glen of Imaals are of no value to the aspiring working terrier-man of today and neither are they of any value as an outcross for the Bedlington, for it is as such that I feel the Glen of Imaal terrier has it's greatest potential.

Perhaps my biggest note of caution regarding using the Glen of Imaal as an outcross is almost the same as George Newcombe's in his choice of lakeland terrier as outcross – selection should be of paramount importance and failure to do so may result in mongrelly progeny. Even in some pure Glen litters I have seen terribly uneven pups showing as much variance as some litters of Jack Russell type terriers. It has been found that 100% Irish stock Glen of Imaals, especially the smaller type, are without a doubt the best proposition for either working or outcrossing.

The first cross Bedlington/Glen of Imaal produces dogs with lots of substance, in some cases too much, easy to understand when one considers the average Glen of Imaal is approximately 13–14 inches high and 28–35 pounds in weight. These dogs despite not being the real heavyweights of their tribe are none the less heavyweights by working terrier standards. First cross dogs paired back to a Bedlington, are probably the best bet for an outcross programme; these three-quarter-bred Bedlingtons are very near to old-type Bedlingtons and Dandie Dinmonts.

Robert Penrose of Manchester has a three-quarter-bred of the kind just described, and this young dog is a real cracker. Easily spannable and with a terrific powerful head, he is the type of Rothbury Forest Bedlington that is not normally seen today. I have yet to see a liver-coloured dog as dark as he is. Time will prove his worth as a working terrier. The father of this dog is a powerful Dandie type owned by Jackie Ison, which was bred by crossing a Glen of Imaal with a predominately Gutchcommon Bedlington, and was mated to George Newcombe's pure-bred registered Bedlington bitch Donna, who was loaned out so that the breeding programme involving the Glen of Imaal as an outcross could be pursued, which thanks to George's generosity it has been. The resulting pups from Donna however were anything but Dandie Dinmont types, being, despite Donna's substance (a sturdy type of bitch) very racy and lithe. A bitch called Red from this pairing is every bit a Bedlington, her only Glen of Imaal characteristics are her courage, coat, and huge jaws and teeth, she generally represents great progress in the pursuit of the true working Bedlington.

Two people whom I have known for several years and always got on very well with are John and Sheila Piggin who, like Roy Mee of Leicester, knew Mrs Williamson quite well and used to visit her farm in Wales.

John not only kept and bred some nice Gutchcommon-line Bedlingtons, he was not against experimental outcrosses as well; in fact, it was John who initially expressed the idea of a Glen of Imaal outcross. After seeing a Glen he turned to Shiela and said, 'Imagine one of these put to a Bedlington and then again back to a Bedlington a second time.' Neither was John (a council pest-control officer) against crossing to fell or lakeland type terriers, he did however voice doubts about the border as an outcross, stating that progeny might well be too short in jaw and leg.

The border terrier outcross

Meanwhile, back in North Yorkshire, George Newcombe was making good progress with both his three-quarter bred Bedlington/lakeland hybrids and also with a new idea, an hybrid twixt Bedlington and border terrier. The ageing Rillington first cross dog Norman, a result of those early outcrossing days between a Bedlington and a lakeland, had produced a number of pups, by both hybrids and pure-bred Bedlingtons. George had allowed Norman to mate John Piggin's Lena (a registered pure-bred Bedlington and sister to the late Roy Mee's well-known brood bitch Bridget of Jarome). From the Norman cross Lena pairing, George gained his blue and tan bitch Venus, Les Robinson had already bought from a previous similarly bred litter, a bitch which he named Amy. This bitch was very near the type of Bedlington desired, with one exception – her size, for she stood all of 19 inches at the shoulder.

Despite this handicap, Les assured me that the bitch would fly to ground on foxes, on earths that she could get to ground on that is, proving that if shoulders and fronts are narrow enough, legs can be folded. This is something I find myself having to explain time and time again, especially to the pro-Russell enthusiasts living in my locality, who just cannot see this. Their very small dogs in many cases not only posess Queen Anne type legs, but also have broad, almost bull terrier-type width and I am fairly sure such animals are suitable only for bushing rabbits.

Before his death, Norman sired other pups for George Newcombe, one real cracker being Ringo (half brother to the three-quarter Glen of Imaal outcross Red), bred from Gallants Nomad, otherwise more popularly known as Donna. This real little miniature of a blue dog certainly looks the part at least, as he is only about 14½ to 15 inches high and none of him is frail, again another example of progress due to outcross. At the time of writing, Bob Istead, a good friend of George Newcombe and also residing in Rillington, has tried a variation on the outcross theme generally practised (that is to say first and second cross matings) by pairing a

A three-quarter Bedlington/quarter Glen of Imaal.

The Irish Glen of Imaal terrier.

bitch he obtained off George, a first cross border Bedlington to the three-quarter bred Ringo.

Initially bred out of a pedigree Bedlington bitch of his own named Dally paired to a red border terrier dog, a dog George kept back out of this union called Dan is really living up to everything George expected of him, being similar in nature to his half brother, the liver-coloured Tarka, and every bit as athletic and agile. If he makes as good a Bedlington type as Tarka he will not be too bad at all. As previously mentioned the border is a related breed to the Bedlington, so must be deemed therefore a useful outcross.

I believe such progeny, five eighths Bedlington, a quarter border and one eighth lakeland have great potential, again time will see whether my optimism is justified or not. People have also produced seven eighths Bedlington/ one eighth outcross.

The fell terrier outcross

Quite apart from the outcrossing programmes I have outlined, others have been tried. Recently a young man from the Chester region wrote to me with an interesting accompanying photograph showing three terriers with a good bag of dead rats. One of the terriers was a first cross Bedlington/black fell terrier. While not criticising the black fell terrier at all (as a matter of fact I admire these dogs), one would need to be very careful with a dog this way bred, as some, though not all, could well be bred from non-coloured dogs, that is to say white-bodied dogs, and again while not criticising the white-bodied Russell types in the least, it is incorrect to have this breeding present in any serious coloured terrier breeding programme, be that Bedlington, lakeland or border.

As an example of how easy it is to breed a coloured terrier from a white-bodied terrier perhaps the following tale will be of interest. A person who was just passing through dogs (and haven't we all met them?) had aquired a 'free to a good home' smooth fox terrier bitch. When the bitch came in season, this person wanted a litter of pups from it, with a long-legged terrier as the sire, and used a liver Gutchcommon-bred Bedlington. Of the resulting pups, three were black and one was red fawn in colour. Later on, when one of the pups changed hands at a Country Fair, I overheard it's new owner refer to it as a patterdale and that he intended to mate it to a lakeland in the future. My bet is, if this pairing took place such animals (½ lakeland, ¼ fox terrier and ¼ Bedlington terrier) would be described as fell terriers.

A situation is now beginning to exist where any black, brown or black and tan terrier is termed a fell terrier, very similar to the situation that exists in some so-called Jack Russell types. Some people really do exploit the situation and sadly more often than not it is the newcomer who comes off the victim, obtaining what to all intents and purposes is a dock-tailed mongrel. Just whether the black fell cross Bedlington hybrid could contribute anything to the cause of the working Bedlington is dubious I think, and it is sadly a cross I'd be careful of, though a controlled programme of trial matings could make the picture a little clearer.

Bedlingtons of course are perfectly alright to use on Russell or black fell terrier bitches to breed working terriers, as long as it's not in a bid to improve the Bedlington. Those fox terrier cross Bedlington hybrids were as good little pups as I had ever seen and I felt would have made good working terriers eventually. Les Robinson of South Humberside, a great enthusiast of both the Bedlington and Bedlington lurcher has a three-quarter bred Jack Russell quarter Bedlington terrier, bred I am told by Bert Gripton, that is an excellent worker.

The Dandie Dinmont outcross

Despite the efforts of Dave Parsons, George Newcombe and myself, none of us has ever found any genuine working strain Dandie Dinmonts. All are apparently show bred and most are as decadent work-wise as show-bred Bedlingtons. Alfred Rhodes' dogs are the most notable exception, pictures of his bitch Misty show a very nice type of Dandie indeed, the kind desired as a possible outcross for the Bedlington. I have no doubt that if the right kind of Dandie could be found it would be a useful addition indeed to the list of suitable outcrosses for the Bedlington.

Why outcross?

What is needed is for more people to try sensible outcrossing on the lines I have indicated and not rely on other people doing it for them, as in the long run, the breed (if the outcrossing has been correctly monitored) will benefit from a greatly expanded gene-pool. Certainly it is the only way of creating new strains and lines, as breeding within the breed's confines is only emulating someone else's work, or diluting working strains with show blood. Having said that, I see the need for keeping the existing pure-bred working strain lines alive and healthy. Perhaps one should consider, whatever outcross line one decides on, what you are trying to put back in the Bedlington. Is it coat, size-reduction, added jaw-power or temperament? Perhaps if it is size or coat, a

29

decent lakeland might start you off on the right foot; you may be trying to put jaw-power and temperament back, if so, perhaps a good first cross Bedlington/Glen of Imaal ot border might suffice. Whatever you decide, just be careful you are conversant with your outcrosses breeding and under no circumstances use suspect lines, to do this is really defeating the object of the excercise.

However, outcrossing is not without snags, as there is always a danger of someone breeding a type which is out of keeping with the Bedlington of old; the mind boggles at how many different types of Bedlington would be around if some of the suggestions one occasionally hears for possible outcrosses were to be put into practice. This is why I have always thought that the idea which the Working Type Bedlington Terrier Association had initially of registering Bedlington hybrids that conformed only to a written standard was a good one. The standard was one for the old-fashioned dog and dogs failing to meet these specifications would not be registered or logged in the stud book, whichever way one cared to term it. It was an idea which sadly never got off the ground and a great pity it was too, as I feel it would have benefited all, if it had done so.

The pure-bred Bedlington

Not everyone who is a genuine supporter of the working Bedlington, as opposed to the person who uses working-type as an advertising slogan, is of the opinion that the dog can be saved only by outcrossing. Mrs Margaret Williamson of Neath, who died in 1984, was one of the breed's stalwarts and fiercely defended her dogs as the only genuine working-type Bedlingtons. Certainly her Gutchcommon-bred dogs were definitely not a modern show type, and I for one have never seen a show-type Bedlington ever, that could compare with a Gutchcommon-bred dog coatwise, both in colour and texture. Not all Gutchcommon dogs were small, by any stretch of the imagination, although evidence does tend to suggest that in her latter years this was the situation with Mrs Williamson's strain; indeed the biggest criticism that I think can be levelled against the Gutchcommon strain is exactly this, especially so in some of the bitches.

Bedlingtons need to be not just small, they need to be robust enough to operate underground to a fox in the way they favour, closing and giving no ground. Mrs Williamson was one of those people who were vehemently against cross-breeding, just as was the late Roy Mee of Leicester who unlike Mrs Williamson, I knew very

30

well. After Mrs Williamson's death Roy obtained all her Bedlingtons' pedigrees, and with his passing I cannot truthfully say what has happened to them. Certainly, Mrs Williamson and Roy Mee bred Bedlingtons that were Gutchcommon through and through and bred this strain exclusively to all others.

Perhaps the most famous of the Gutchcommon Bedlington terriers is one of the early ones, namely Worton Demon. Apparently bred by Mrs Williamson in 1923 and sired by Goxhill Blue Boy, the dog was a typical example of the Gutchcommon Bedlington in their heyday. Just as a matter of interest, Mrs Williamson established Worton as a prefix in 1926; as to why she gave it up and adopted Gutchcommon seems a little uncertain.

I have indicated that Mrs Williamson bred dogs quite closely, and an example of this was a bitch she gave away to George Newcombe that was born in 1964 and named Jenny Wren of Gutchcommon. From this Bedlington's pedigree it appears that Mrs Williamson started off with a dog named George of Winfield which she renamed Robby of Gutchcommon. Mrs Williamson used Robby of Gutchcommon 10 times and four times mated brother to sister. The only other addition was Lena of Gutchcommon who was a quarter bred Gutchcommon by Robby of Gutchcommon. Since then Mrs Williamson used Dick of Gutchcommon quite extensively (bred by Dave Roberts). Other additions included Blythe Blue Red Rover once, and Argonauts Blue Pierrette.

When Mrs Williamson died, Roy Mee of Leicester took over as it were, where she had left off; even one of the last dogs he bred showed relics of Mrs Williamson's past breeding programme. A litter of pups bred by Roy, showed Dick of Gutchcommon six times being used and five times Rusty of Gutchcommon. Likewise Dick of Gutchcommon is found six times in the pedigree of The Mad Ratter. However, it was neither Mrs Williamson nor Roy Mee who instigated this, though I suspect they would have approved. In the case of The Mad Ratter, the dog in question was sound and was used as the base line for the newly emerging Strike line of working-type Bedlington.

I fear that not everyone can gel with the nature of a Gutchcommon Bedlington and this in turn has led to perhaps some unjust criticism. I have found them to be in the vein of some border terriers, a little slow to start, they certainly do not like to be pushed into working, preferring to do it slowly and in their own time. This has also led me to disagree with George Newcombe during our regular correspondence to each other. When I have stated that Bedlington terriers are slow to work, he has disagreed, stating that

A border terrier.

(Gallants Nomad) Donna.

his Rillington-bred Bedlingtons have always been fast to start work and never needed much in the way of encouragement.

Perhaps the biggest difference between the Gutchcommon and Rillington strains of Bedlington is their nature. Physical differences are also apparent in varying degrees, such as a rounded bottom jaw in the case of a Rillington-bred Bedlington (it is rather pointed in most Gutchcommon-bred Bedlingtons), and size, Rillingtons tending to be that shade bigger, though probably this makes them more of what George would term 'a viable moor dog', (The North Yorkshire moors being the countryside around the village of Rillington would make this a preference.)

The late Roy Mee's two most famous Gutchcommon-bred Bedlingtons were both litter brothers and Registered as Kentenes Rogue and Rogue of Birkacre (otherwise known as Buzzer and Rex) and they certainly did their fair share of siring many puppies, in the Midlands regions. They figured extensively in recent Gutchcommon pedigrees, through their dam Gutchcommon Russett (as her name suggests, a liver-coloured bitch) who in turn was sired by Gutchcommon Rusty, one of those extensively used dogs of Mrs Williamson. (Also of note is Gutchcommon Russett's dam, Blue Bonnett of Gutchcommon, who in turn was sired by the well-used Dick of Gutchcommon bred by Dave Roberts.)

Buzzer and Rex also figured in some modern show-type dogs though possibly the show-type animals may have been owned by people who wished to work them and wanted to bring in working blood when they bred from them. Whatever the case, Gutchcommon blood has been used extensively for many years now and widely bred in some cases to modern show-type animals. Puppies from these unions have been bought in turn by working enthusiasts, who probably bought in haste and repented at leisure. Not all Gutchcommon cross show-type matings were through ignorance however, I personally know one show breeder who went out of his way to use a Gutchcommon-bred dog to improve coat, improve coat it certainly did – pity it was not registered though – enough said!

In a letter sent to *Shooting News*, Fiona Craig, a show enthusiast and member of the Bedlington Terrier Association actually stated that both she and Ken Bounden the club's chairman, had shown Gutchcommon stock at championship shows. I know this to be true as reliable sources have told me that Fiona Craig had a dog from Mrs Williamson which was shown with some success; however it was sometimes failed for having insufficient leg hair.

Perhaps the last paragraph will illustrate to the reader how

utterly at opposites the show and working enthusiasts are – to a
working terrier enthusiast, how can a dog have insufficient leg
hair? Especially when one considers these leg furnishings are
pathetically soft and woolly and, at the correct length the show
judges look for, such a furnished dog would be reduced to a
matted, tangled wreck within half an hour's mink hunting – no, five
minutes might be a more correct assessment. Can you imagine such
a dog working to a fox in a damp clay condition? My advice is, if you
have a Bedlington with leg furnishings and you do intend to work
him, do yourself and your dog a favour – clip such furnishings off.

From the reports one gets from time to time from reliable
sources up and down the country it seems the Bedlington is getting
a fair old crack of the whip from hunters. Recently I heard of one
Bedlington who went to ground on a private estate where the
landowner had been keen to get rid of the fox that had been taking
just a few too many pheasants for his liking. He had asked his
game-keeper if he had got the fox yet? The keeper said yes, not
daring to admit that his Russell had quit after a fair old tussle below
ground. He then went back to his cottage, and got out his year-old
blue Bedlington dog whose only experience with foxes had been
ragging very dead shot ones, and returned with it to the earth.
Upon smelling the vulpine perfume around the earth and below
ground, the dog went below with a locator on, the keeper waited
and soon it became obvious it was a digging job.

After six hours and darkness falling, the keeper and under-
keeper eventually reached a dead fox and then another and
eventually the dog, right up to his third fox (all in one earth). That
was from a very tight place and despite blows raining down on the
youngster he still stayed to his quarry. On his way to a nearby public
house the owner of the land noticed a light in the field where the
keepers were and upon going to investigate he was so pleased when
they told him the young dog had just killed two and worked a third
fox that he quite forgot the fox from that earth had supposedly
already been accounted for. Whether he remembered later or not I
do not know.

For handy little dogs, one need look no further than John
Piggins Bedlingtons, as these are worked daily with John as a pest
control officer with Newark Council, and the stories John has of his
exploits, especially with old Jasper of Kentene, would fill a book in
itself. All of his dogs, Jasper, Floyd, Lena and Gemma are as
familiar figures at the council depot yard as John is himself. George
Newcombe's dogs were once a familiar sight out with the
Saltersgate Hunt, doubling as ferreting dogs back home in the

week, and many other Bedlingtons in this country and also abroad are now being seen as working terriers, and gaining opportunities to prove themselves.

That the Bedlington terrier of old can still be found and the fact he will survive is incentive enough, then let him come forth and show himself for what he is – a working terrier quite unique in both his temperament and his physique. Let him show the world that, for all his appearance, he truly is the 'Lion in the Lamb'.

The Rillington Bedlington

The story of George's first Bedlington, a bitch registered as Sheila of Grovedale with the Kennel Club and simply known as Sheila to George, was purchased in 1946 from Mr Hammond of Kirby Moorside upon George's return from the army after the Second World War, for the princely sum of £5. This amount had been given to him and all the ex-servicemen of the village returning from the war. Prior to this, George had never had working terriers and since that time has only ever owned Bedlington and lakeland terriers, both of which are prefixed Rillington after the place where he now lives, the only exception to this I believe, has been a couple of pet beagles which were his daughter's.

So began the family of Rillington. An interesting fact is that, sometimes through several different lines, all George's present-day Bedlingtons can be traced back to this original Bedlington bitch. George bred Sheila to the sire Sudston Panda and kept back a dog pup, registered as Dauntless Dingo, Kennel name Dingo, which was bred to a bitch called Burleydene Blue Mantle which was called by the name of Lindy back at home.

The resulting pup, Rillington Rinty is one George remembers with affection and was the basis for the Rillington strain as we know it today. Rinty, to quote George, 'Was a wolf in sheeps clothing' and a more hard-bitten game dog George has not since owned. Stories of Rinty's aggressive, uncompromising nature are numerous indeed; the dog was said by George, to fear nothing and that included humans as well as animals. When I visited Rillington in July 1986, George said to me of his old warrior, 'He feared nothing John, another dog had only got so much as to look at him and he'd have it, and when he was in a temper, he'd have me as well, he feared nothing, man nor beast'.

Even as a pup Rinty had found trouble, but a leg crippled through a puppyhood fight did nothing to deter the young Rinty. Later on when he was worked, he did so in grim deathly silence.

35

Upon entering a fox earth Rinty would get up to his fox, once there he killed it or drew it. Rinty's daughter Rillington Rarity and her son Rillington Rustler both in later years adopted the same ruthless way of working, supporting George's theory that fox-drawing dogs are born, not made. Rinty could be regarded as a relic from the bygone age – the age of the real Bedlington's, and certainly gave one very lucky Yorkshireman a glimpse into that bygone era.

When I interviewed George Newcombe informerly at my house in November 1986, I asked him what was his best Bedlington ever. George sat back into his chair, drew on his Senior Service and thought. After a slight pause, he stared back at me and said, 'That's a hard one John, for there's been so many good dogs over the years and all had different qualities, I so admired'. Again George paused, 'however if I had to say who was the hardest one ever that's easy – Rinty'.

Only people who have owned over the many years, great individual working dogs with characters to match, will know how stunningly accurate that statement of Mr Newcombe's was. I remember asking him a similar question back in Rillington in the summer of that year – which was his favourite present dog. It was a question George could not answer – admittedly he had some choice (14 terriers in all), though I suspect he had a soft spot for Norman his first cross Bedlington/lakeland, and I know, it was a very sad day indeed for George when the warrior had to be put peacefully to sleep.

From the union of Rillington Rinty and Tynefield Amoret came Rillington Rarity otherwise known as Darkie, Darkie also worked in the same ruthless manner as his illustrious and uncompromising sire Rinty, and when eventually George decided to breed with her she was paired to her half-brother Rillington Rip, bred from Burleydene Tiny Tim and Darkie's dam, Tynefield Amoret. There is, as it happens a rather nice story concerning Tynefield Amoret (better known as Sheba to George) which illustrates the ample fire and guts the show dogs still had in those immediate post-war years. One day with the Sallersgate Hunt Sheba was put to ground on a big dog fox. After a considerable dig, the diggers reached the bitch which, when George examined her, had her top jaw broken in two places, but the bitch was so fired up that she was still raring to go if only George had allowed her to, and all this from a Bedlington that George bought from Northumberland at the age of three years old that had never done any kind of work prior to him owning her.

With the Rillington Rip/Rarity pairing, george bred Rillington Rustler, a puppy he named Trigger, that was paired to the bitch

Gay otherwise registered under the name of Rillington Rapture. Gay was by Northcote Terpo, the last time George introduced show breeding, (approximately 20 years ago from the time of writing) a dog that was bred from show champion parents. The dam of Gay was Rillington Really Blue, a bitch George named Smokey and one he described as the only real blue he had ever seen (hence the appropriate name Really Blue) who was in turn sired by a dog named Flint. Flint or Rillington Ranger was sired by Dick of Gutchcommon bred by Dave Roberts and out of a bitch called Promise registered as Jenny Wren of Gutchcommon who was given to George by Margaret Williamson. Smokey's dam was Rillington Rarity. Rillington Rustler and Really Blue were half brother and sister.

Eventually Rustler and Rapture were paired together to produce Rillington Resolute a dog known as Gallant and a very significant one in Rillington terms as he was George's most direct link with his (to use George's own words) 'old Line'. When George eventually used a liver dog called Gutchcommon George to Rillington Really Blue, he produced a liver bitch with a particularly good coat both in texture and colour, the bitch Rillington Ruby Red, when paired to Gallant (Rillington Resolute) produced George's present-day pure bred, Kennel Club registered Bedlingtons.

By now however, George was voicing an opinion that outcrossing was essential, and met with snide remarks behind his back, all of which he was aware of. One person was known to have said of Rillington Ruby Red, she cannot possibly be pure bred with a coat like that. Reader, beware if you embark on outcrossing, or even just voice an opinion that it might be beneficial to the breed or type; to do so, you too will be subjected to such remarks by the purists, especially if you have a litter of pure bred pups at the time (think about it).

From the Rillington Ruby Red cross Gallant union came Gallants Nimrod, (called Blue) and Donna. Donna bred the Strike-bred bitch Gold Strike, by the sire First Strike – Jackie Ison's Sam, a first cross Bedlington/Glen of Imaal, who in turn was sired by The Mad Ratter bred by John Piggin of Eakring, Nottinghamshire. The Mad Ratter has links with Rillington Resolute though very very distantly; he (Gallant) is one of Ratters great, great grandparents). Dally (a blue bitch and litter sister to Donna and Blue) is the dam of George's Dan (his new outcross line by a red border terrier dog) as is Tarka a particularly good liver coloured dog sired by George's Turk, a blue and tan lakeland-type terrier.

Through Lena, John Piggin's blue bitch, his own Donna, and

another bitch out of Dally and the lakeland Turk, George has considerably developed his own outcrossing line from the lakeland. George's kennel now has three-quarter bred bitches – Venus by Lena and Norman, and Dart by a first cross blue bitch and the old dog Gallant (a grandfather to grand daughter mating), and also it's cousin the good little type of dog Ringo by Norman and Donna.

Amy, a bitch, blue and tan in colour and bred by John Piggin out of his bitch Lena and Norman, showed that size variance can occur in outcrossing, not in actual fact that this should be of a major concern, as selection and line breeding can correct this. Amy was bought as a puppy by Les Robinson of Brigg and although 19 inches high was a great type of bitch for producing lurchers; I gather Les had considerable success when he paired Amy to Cowdells Willhay a first cross whippet/greyhound and a dog with quite a reputation as a speed merchant. Amy however is not just a running dog base-line, Les works her and only recently wrote to me, saying Amy has entered to fox with relish. Of course, assuming the earth is large enough, this does support the statement that if fronts and shoulders are correct, legs can be folded.

George Newcombe is not only famous for his Bedlington terriers, he is also well known for his interest and enthusiasm for the old-fashioned lakeland terrier, and was one of the terriermen featured in Brian Plummer's very deep and informative book *The Fell Terrier*. Regarding George's comments on the true old-fashioned lakeland I have heard him called controversial and even hypercritical. He is, I feel justifiably very critical of some of today's dogs known as lakelands, in fact in the contemplation of a lakeland as an outcross, George said to me, 'I would say it is far easier for the average person to find a suitable border to use than a lakeland'.

Constantly George has written to me referring to lakelands, a typical example is the following quote, 'I would be very sceptical of any dog which had a smooth short coat and white tipped feet or white nails. The exception to this is the dog who really looks like a lakeland and has the true iron-hard long-haired outer coat, but which due to the lack of undercoat, it lies flat to the skin instead of standing out as it should do'.

Certainly when the terrier shows became so very popular in the Midlands, my immediate reaction to some of the varying types were, so many are dock-tailed mongrels, the exceptions being some of the blacks commonly referred to, though rather inaccurately, as patterdales (in fact quite a lot of black fell terrier lines are now breeding relatively true to type) and some lakeland types. Many

38

Working type Bedlingtons.

Two Bedlington bitches.

coloured terriers are however mongrels and really do justify this description.

An absolute gem just has to be related at this point. One lady overheard talking to another at a working terrier show, first lady says, 'What is your dog?' Second lady, very pleased that someone is interested says, 'It's a border lakeland patterdale Russell'. Yes, well that about covers them all, so somewhere along the line she should be at least part correct.

Other working Bedlington lines

Despite many rumours from several different sources that other working lines or families of Bedlingtons exist, none has yet surfaced. Brian Plummer, in his book *Rogues and Running Dogs* speaks of a strain of Bedlington terriers, probably pure-bred that exists in Wales, but despite extensive enquiries by certain individuals, no one has ever been able to find this family, including people who have spent quite some time in Wales specifically in pursuit of this elusive strain.

Dave Parsons, whom I believe now lives a life wandering the waterways of Kent, and is something of an expert on genetics, believed or hoped that an unknown strain existed somewhere in the valleys of Wales. Despite the fact that Bedlingtons are very popular in Wales, I think there is about as much chance of finding an unknown strain of Bedlington in Wales as there is in England. Dave Roberts's Garth Forest dogs offered probably the best chance of that elusive strain as Roberts, a former regional officer and Assistant Secretary to the Working Bedlington Terrier Club hailed from Whitchurch in Cardiff, Wales. (Roberts incidentally bred Dick of Gutchcommon as has already been stated.) Despite this I do not think another working strain exists in Wales.

Other suggested outcrosses

Some rare old suggestions get made regarding suitable outcrosses even though the ones suggested already are far and away good enough for a potentially expanded gene-pool. As I say, some are best left in the vivid imaginations of the people who suggest them as they really are jokes indeed. Mind you a consistently suggested outcross is the Kerry blue terrier, the Kerry probably the most recent created of the four Irish terriers is obviously related one way or another to the Glen of Imaal, as are the other two Irish breeds.

Despite this, where do you find small working Kerrys? Most nowadays are large show dogs, although enthusiasts of the Kerry blue terrier point out their wards' blind courage is still apparent despite the handicap of a show career. Perhaps they are right, as quite a number of Kerry blue cross greyhounds are now making a fair old name for themselves as fox-hunting lurchers, especially so in mainland Britain. As a footnote to the suggestion of the Kerry blue terrier as an outcross to the Bedlington, perhaps it should be remembered that Kerry blues are remarkably thick-skinned terriers, a quality one should bear in mind in the production of either a working terrier or lurcher.

Now the time has come to finish this chapter and concentrate on one of the people who have championed the cause of the real Bedlington, a person who is very much the main man at present, the real champion of the breed in recent times, Mr George Newcombe.

—4—

George Newcombe

THE VERY MENTION of the name George Newcombe is synonymous with the working Bedlington terrier and in particular George's own Rillington-bred Bedlingtons. Born in Burrell, near Beedale in 1918, George Newcombe is a true Yorkshireman through and through and a more friendly person no one could ever wish to meet. Of course George, apart from gaining a reputation for being controversial (something I doubt I've done anything to lessen) in his views on lakelands and being a staunch critic like myself of the modern show-type Bedlington, is also well known for his involvement with the first working club for Bedlingtons.

Subsequently George became the club's first chairman; however after a sequence of events, George quit the post and was answerable only to himself in his choice of different dogs for his breeding programme. Perhaps this is a significant consideration we should bear in mind when we witness how successful George Newcombe has been in reviving the true Bedlington. Another point of significance we should be aware of is that at a meeting of the Working Bedlington Terrier Club a proposal was put forward that the club should organise show classes, on the basis (and one I might add I don't agree with) that it would be good publicity for the breed to do so. However, a counter proposal was made, stating it was not the function of a club whose objective was solely to breed the working type Bedlingtons to organise show classes and that in any case there were insufficient dogs around of the right type for it to gain good publicity, and the original proposal was dropped.

However, various working terrier shows (just as the current trend is today) did put on classes for Bedlingtons and George

Newcombe and a friend of his from York attended several of these events and found that not a single judge handled the dogs as though they knew what they were looking for in a Bedlington. I believe many judges today are rather slung in at the deep end at working terrier shows and on one occasion I was asked by a petrified young chap already judging the coloured and white terriers at a show if I would judge the Bedlingtons there that day. I might add that there were only two, so he had at least 50 per cent chance of getting the decision right. But as you have probably guessed, he blew it, and yet admitted to me afterwards he had undertaken the judging appointment knowing full well Bedlingtons were scheduled on the day. A plea to all clubs who do stage classes for Bedlingtons at working shows – please get a person who knows what he or she is really looking for, to do otherwise is utterly nonsensical.

Without a doubt, upon the formation of the two clubs that existed for the Bedlington as a working dog, both the original Working Bedlington Terrier Club and the Working Type Bedlington Terrier Association, many people wanted showing to be a major role of the clubs activities. A fact I became aware of was that so many people were prepared to travel several hundred miles to a show where classes were on, yet were not prepared to attend meetings or work their dogs on allotted ground to gain working certificates. If I come across as disillusioned and bitter, then I make no apology, as my experience with working clubs was that people wanted a club, but they did not want to contribute to its existence. In common with George Newcombe, I resigned after having had enough of all the hassle.

Ironically, as I write this, I see yet another move is afoot for the reformation of a working Bedlington club, and a call has gone out for all Bedlington fans to attend the Shropshire Game fair as Bedlington terrier classes are scheduled; I just wonder if the judge will be an established Bedlington enthusiast.

When, several years ago, I wrote to George for the first time and asked him for his opinion on an outcrossing programme, having in mind a cross twixt Bedlington and Glen of Imaal, I was slightly surprised that he was in support of it. Although some had described George to me as sharp and blunt, which I imagine he could be if you crossed him, I found him a very courteous and mild-mannered man, and it was he more than any other outsider, who encouraged me in the dark days when so many people scorned and dismissed my ideas as rubbish. Since that time, George Newcombe has helped me, given me information freely, loaned me a dog Donna (Gallants Nomad) and has taught me so much about life, let alone Bedlington terriers.

Also, George has always been honest with me, and several times we have had to agree to disagree. The underlying truth must be emphasised however, that George has always accepted, even when he does not agree with the said persons, that everyone has a right to voice his opinions. I consider this a fairly good outlook generally and oh, if it could only be that everyone thought this way.

The following is a condensed version of George's first letter to me regarding his opinion on the Glen of Imaal/Bedlington terrier cross.

Dear Mr. Glover,

Thank you for your letter, which I found very interesting and your suggestion of using a Glen of Imaal terrier an unusual one.

I must confess that until I received your letter I really had no knowledge of the Glen of Imaal terrier. I have seen chaps with smooth-coated brindle terriers which they claimed were Glen of Imaal terriers. I am impressed that you are prepared to do something constructive, unlike many people who contact me.

I would be prepared to co-operate with you on the project [which ultimately he did. George's concluding paragraph is also worthy of note and I continue], I can assure you there is no advantage in Kennel Club registration, the only thing it guarantees is that one can exhibit a registered dog at K.C. shows and that stock bred from registered dogs can in turn be registered and eventually shown.

Yours sincerely

George Newcombe

Encouragement indeed, and when Jill of Strike, a blue working Glen of Imaal bitch produced her four pups by The Mad Ratter, a strong liver-coloured Gutchcommon-bred Bedlington, George was there again with the same encouragement.

George continued to follow the progress of the pups and it was Sam, a pup from the progeny, who caught George's eye and was eventually the Sire to Red (Gold Strike) out of George's bitch Donna (Gallants Nomad).

A gentleman who used to correspond and occasionally visit George Newcombe, called Dave Parsons, was also informed via George that a Glen of Imaal could be considered as a possible outcross for the Bedlington. George had sent to Dave Parsons, at the time residing on the waterways of Kent, two photographs of

44

George Newcombe.

The kennel at Rillington.

mine, showing English-bred Glen pups. Dave Parsons, something of an amateur geneticist I believe, thought the cross should be tried, though he did voice doubts as the following quote from one of his letters to me will show.

> "From a study of the photographs that George sent to me, although this could only be really established by trial matings, I would say that the bone structure of the Glen of Imaal was of a different genetical type to that of the Dandies, and therefore not suitable for their production.
>
> Now do not be put off, Mr Glover, by what I have said, as I am talking from the point of view of my own breeding programme, [This is the man who was experimenting with the dachsund outcross] I hope you will continue with your project as I would say that the strength, gameness, length and shape and flexibility of the body of the Glen of Imaal, together with the heavy jaw and hard coat, would be very useful additions to the gene-pool for improved Bedlingtons of the type of John Cornforth's Nelson, a 19th century dog with a very long sprung body, strong, not-too-long legs, and a great strong head on him with massive jaws and teeth. At 15 inches height, Nelson weighed-in at 25 pounds, and with a blue-black coat was a type of dog not seen today – a lovely heavy-weight Bedlington."

Not long after this letter I lost contact with Dave Parsons and neither George Newcombe nor I ever heard from him again. I sometimes read letters in the field sports press from a person in Kent, who writes under a pen name that sounds very Dave Parsonish, so perhaps he is still out there somewhere quietly trying to revive the Bedlington of old, possibly in some narrow-boat on a canal in Kent. If you are, Dave, all the best my friend.

Happily Dave Parsons was found wrong and, with further generations, two types of old Rothbury dogs have been produced from a Glen of Imaal grandparent, namely racey Bedlington types, large jawed and good coated, and flexible light Dandie types.

Of the lakeland/fell terrier cross George said to me, 'Probably the lakeland is really the most logical dog to use in the improvement of the Bedlington, because in the ideal specimens they do have many almost identical characteristics, namely a good strong head, jaw power, big teeth and pendant ears. Both have straight legs, a narrow front and clean, well-laid-back shoulders and the lakeland has a superior coat. There is also the possibility that one may pick up a far distant Bedlington ancestor for, in the early days of the lakeland, Bedlingtons were quite extensively used. In a lakeland/

Bedlington cross, the undesirable features which one gets from a Bedlington viewpoint, are too-small ears, roundness of rib, a too-level back, possibly hardly sufficient body length and too-gay tail carriage. There is though the advantage of being able to revert very easily to the lakeland, as a friend of mine who has Tarka's sister [Tarka is a first cross lakeland/fell/Bedlington hybrid] has done mating his bitch, which produced my three-quarter bred Bedlington bitch (Dart) and the only undesirable feature I can visualise in the progeny of this mating is a coat which will not be a typical lakeland.' The problem George sees for anyone contemplating the lakeland/ bedlington cross is first find your lakeland, and perhaps in the style that has earned George that controversial tag, he concluded, 'A large proportion of the so-called lakelands are in fact mongrels.'

George was equally as honest when it came to the subject of working-Bedlington clubs and I now must agree with what he was saying at the time when the Working-type Bedlington Terrier Association was being formed. When I asked George if he would be interested in the formation of a new club for working Bedlingtons after the apparent collapse of the first club, of which of course George was the initial chairman, his answer was, 'Once bitten twice shy,' and he continued, 'For the last two years various organisations, including our North Yorks Rescue Club, have scheduled Bedlington classes at their working terrier shows. I have attended them, not because I like showing, more because I thought it might help to promote the cause of the working-type Bedlington. My conclusion was that it was a sheer waste of time and money, because none of the judges really knew what they were looking for. This is not a case of sour grapes, as I did my share of winning, in fact probably more so than anyone else, but as far as I could see, it did nothing to encourage the correct type of Bedlington. Much the same applies to the Working Bedlington Terrier Club. I was the original club chairman and I did all I could via the medium of the club magazine to arouse interest and enthusiasm among members for the cause of the working-type Bedlington – and all I met with was apathy. Members were so complacent and, almost without exception, thought the Bedlingtons they had were O.K. and were certainly not prepared to take the necessary measures to breed a universal and correct type of working Bedlington.'

All this has a familiar ring to it for me, for a similar situation existed in the last club, the Working Type Bedlington Terrier Association and I predict that if another club is formed, its fate will be the same. Of the initial club's name, George said, 'The Rothbury

George Newcombe's Grip.

George Newcombe's three-quarter lakeland/ quarter Bedlington.

George Newcombe's first cross Bedlington/lakeland.

Type Bedlington Club' might have been a more logical one, for one of the stated aims of the club, indeed the main one, was to breed the old type of Bedlington. Not that it would have made any real difference to the outcome because members did not have the resolve to take the measures which were necessary to breed the right type of dog. It would however have stopped the stupid practice of calling dogs working-type when quite obviously they were not. After the failure of the club a small number of us decided to try to continue the objective of breeding the old-fashioned Bedlington, but gradually they all dropped out and no serious collective attempts were made to see through the project although a few people such as Dave Parsons and myself did try to do so.

In those early days of the Working Type Bedlington Terrier Association quite a number of people appeared interested in reviving the breed, seeing this as possibly the most logical way of achieving the correct type of dog and I lent myself fully to its formation. George Newcombe also conceded it was the most logical way of reviving interest, but his prediction of the club's eventual demise and his hints as to how I would personaly feel when I resigned from the club and ultimately left it to the devices of the rest of the committee, were a chillingly accurate one. His position which he made very clear was hard for me to understand at the time, yet I find now, I am in full agreement. Of the proposed new club, he said, 'I believe a club or society is the most logical way to try to improve the Bedlington, though perhaps I should make my position clear in the matter. My experience with the last club has made me very sceptical that such an organisation will achieve anything in promoting the cause of the working Bedlington and I just cannot re-kindle the enthusiasm that I had for the first club. It is all very well for people to express an interest but talk is cheap and I am inclined to think that it may be only lip service and that not many of them will take positive action.' This proved to be true.

At the first working terrier show I attended where Bedlington classes were staged, I overheard (though I tend to think I was meant to) a so-called working Bedlington enthusiast say, 'It's all very well crossing, but I think all the dogs should be pure bred and Kennel Club registered.' His attitude was fairly predictable, especially when one saw his dogs, big 17½-inch brutes, probably rabbiting dogs as they were described by him in a letter sent to me earlier as, 'from working families and they do not have any problems picking things up.' Later I had an opportunity to examine his dogs' pedigrees; they were practically all show-type bred, the working breeding they did have being negligible.

This attitude is widespread and is confirmed in a letter George sent me on the 5 July 1985, where he expressed the opinion, 'I think it is significant when so many people are concerned about Kennel Club registration, for obviously they are interest in only the financial side of it and in turn selling their stock as pets, etc.'

Time and time again George Newcombe comes up with something that I find myself in agreement with, like his reference to Bedlingtons catching rabbits on the run. In all the years he has been a Bedlington breeder, George has never seen a Bedlington that could catch a healthy rabbit on its own run in daylight. He sees the rabbit coursing Bedlington stories in the same light as the one he once heard of two Bedlingtons about 11 inches high who always closed with and killed their fox. George continued, 'Whether it was both together or single-handed I do not know. Well, I have had Bedlingtons which could kill a fox single-handed, though they were 16 inch dogs, but where on earth do you find 11 inch midgets capable of this?'

So at this point, I will close this chapter on the doyen of the breed, George Newcombe, and although there will be further reference to him in this book, let me say no finer ambassador of the real and true Bedlington terrier exists.

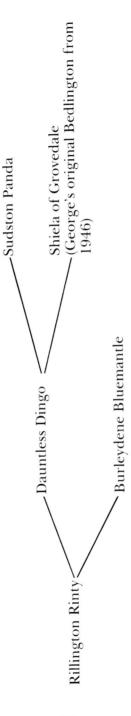

The Pedigree of Rillington Rinty, owned and bred by George Newcombe

Sudston Panda

Shiela of Grovedale
(George's original Bedlington from 1946)

Dauntless Dingo

Burleydene Bluemantle

Rillington Rinty

The Pedigree of Rillington Ruby Red, owned and bred by George Newcombe

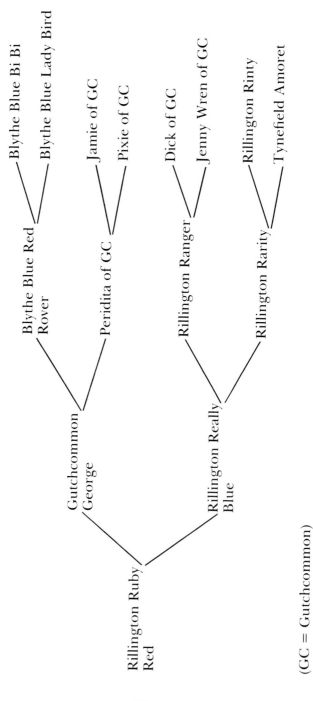

(GC = Gutchcommon)

—5—

Margaret Williamson

ANY BOOK ON the working Bedlington terrier would not be complete without a chapter on a person who was undoubtedly one of the great champions of the cause, namely Mrs Margaret Williamson, who bred her own beloved Gutchcommon Bedlingtons. Mrs Williamson spent at least 60 years of her long life championing what she believed to be the real Bedlington (the old-fashioned type).

There is absolutely no doubt that Mrs Williamson was an intelligent person who knew exactly what she wanted from a Bedlington. It is equally certain that some people criticised Margaret's breeding policies but no person ever did more to promote the working Bedlington than Margaret did.

Although Mrs Williamson spent many of her years living at Bryncock Farm near Neath, South Wales, it appears that Mrs Williamson and her base stock hailed originally from the South of England. Gutchcommon, I believe, is a common in Devonshire and most certainly Devonshire was the home of the Misses Maunsell and Hamilton, the source from whence this ex-school teacher obtained the early beginnings of her strain. The Misses Maunsell and Hamilton along with Mrs Williamson liked the same type of dog, namely a workmanlike lathy dog with a good jacket on it; sadly so many modern-day Bedlingtons do not conform to this description.

I have heard show people remark that Violet Maunsell and her friend Dorothy Hamilton were bloodthirsty admirers of working Bedlingtons. Like Mrs Williamson they were at one time show-judges and held in very high esteem. Without doubt, Violet and Dorothy were a major influence on the aspiring champion, Margaret. However, to find the source of the family Gutchcommon, one must go back even further than Violet Maunsell and Dorothy Hamilton's dogs, back to the family of Bedlingtons known as Sparkeforde, a prefix held by one Major E.B. Aylward who bred in 1911 a Bedlington called Sparkeforde Jackanapes, a superb dog who not only conformed to all the basic requisites one would desire in a working Bedlington, but a dog who gained the title of show bench Champion, and in those days in the early part of the century dogs were frequently found who could justifiably claim the now almost mythical distinction of being dual-purpose (working and show dogs). In fact the Misses Maunsell and Hamilton advertised their dog Heart of Hell at stud as a showdog who held a working certificate (and oh, if it were only so today).

Nevertheless, Bellerby Surprise was mated to Sparkeforde Jill and Sparkeforde Jackanapes (otherwise known as Jackie) was the resulting blue and tan Bedlington from the union (although he was registered with the Kennel Club as a solid blue for some reason or other). Mrs Williamson remembered well Jackanapes and even in her winter years still recalled this blue and tan Bedlington with great fondness. Over the telephone a year or two before her death, Margaret described Jackie to me, as a true Blue and Tan, with a good neck, good shoulders, tail set correct, perfect feet, standing around 16 inches high, with a long, strong, slim head and set off with a dark eye. You will not find many dogs of his ilk today. Mrs Williamson also claimed Jackie could be found in virtually all good Bedlington pedigrees. Her admiration of this Bedlington was very evident and quite easy to understand when one knows he was the sire of Mrs Williamson's Musha, the famous dam of the equally famous and perhaps arguably the best of all the Gutchcommon Bedlingtons, Worton Demon.

Mrs Williamson had bought the bitch Musha from the Misses Maunsell and Hamilton in 1923 and it was these two ladies who owned Sparkeforde Jackanapes latterly jointly, though firstly by Miss Violet Maunsell. Through Worton Demon's sire Goxhill Blue Boy one can trace all the way back to the very beginning of Bedlington history. One should be under no doubt that Mrs Margaret Williamson's dogs were unquestionably the true old-fashioned type. George of Wynfield, bought in after the Second World War by Mrs Williamson was traced back also directly to the original dogs through his ancestor Worton Demon. I know this to be true as Roy Mee, a person who I knew very well up to his death in November 1987, had Robby of Gutchcommon's (which is what Mrs Williamson re-named him) Kennel Club registration card.

Over the subsequent years Mrs Williamson bred her Bedlingtons mainly within the confines of her own strain as quite simply she did not believe there to be a strain of Bedlington anywhere to compare with her beloved Gutchcommon-bred dogs. However, one would be misled if one believed she stuck to this principle rigidly; additions, although quite rare, did exist. Dick of Gutchcommon, Blythe Blue Red Rover and Argonauts Blue Pierette are Bedlingtons that spring to mind that Mrs Williamson used within her strain of dogs.

Roy Mee, of Whetstone, near Leicester was a great friend of Mrs Williamson, certainly during the last six years of her life, and I know Roy visited her on occasions weekly and almost certainly every holiday and in fact, it was through Roy that I got to see many all Gutchcommon-bred Bedlington terriers. Many of these contemporary Gutchcommons carried all the qualities one needed for a working dog like, coat and guts, and they were not frail either. In fact on occasions, I thought some fell into the category of too-big just to prove that all Gutchcommon dogs are not small or frail, which is what some of the critics of the strain think, or say, or perhaps both. As a spin-off, some of the outsize Gutchcommons would have been ideal stud dogs to greyhounds to produce viable all-round working lurcher dogs. Incidently, just prior to Roy Mee's unfortunate death this gentleman owned a superb largish Gutchcommon dog with a terrific coat, and I make no secret ot it, I often wondered who obtained it after Roy's demise.

I do like the Gutchcommon Bedlingtons, they will and do work, they are gutsy enough to work fox, their coats are in a different world to other dogs and it is a great legacy one ex-school teacher left the world of the working Bedlington.

Nevertheless, I would be wrong to say everyone felt that the Gutchcommon Bedlington terrier was as good and viable a dog as I do. For there are critics of the strain and oddly enough they are not all show people either – in fact, quite the reverse may well be nearer the truth. Certainly the Gutchcommon prefix was familiar to show people; Fiona Craig, Ken Bounden and Alice Emsley, all show enthusiasts of many years standing are all familiar with the family Gutchcommon and Mrs Curran Cooper of Beverley was an avid admirer of the working-type dogs Mrs Williamson bred, and knew and respected the views of Mrs Williamson and the Misses Maunsell and Hamilton.

I believe Mrs Curran Cooper and Mrs Williamson co-operated closely at one time in breeding the correct type of Bedlington and certainly a dog I saw that was reputedly due to this co-operation showed immense promise. There is no doubt that Mrs Williamson

A typical Gutchcommon bred Bedlington.

A Bedlington containing Gutchcommon breeding.

was aware that the show fraternity wanted to use her dogs to improve coats in the present show stock, at least some of them did. Of this practice, she said to me during a telephone call, 'If a show person wishes to use one of my stud-dogs, they may; all I will say is this – it will improve their puppies' coats immensely.'

It seems that when any person achieves anything of note, be it in livestock, flowers, gardening or sport, there is always somebody there waiting to criticise. Many years ago a friend of my father said about his prize-winning exhibition border canaries, 'When they stop talking about and criticising my birds then I'll worry.' To some Mrs Williamson could just not do any right, their condemnation and criticism of the strain was immense and yet, if it was so bad, how did it reach such a peak in the 1960s and 1970s? (Yes, I am aware that some may question those as vintage Gutchcommon years.)

Perhaps the biggest criticism in the later years of Mrs Williamson's life was aimed at the amount of in-breeding and line-breeding she had allowed within the strain. Stories circulated around of moody, sulky little dogs with bad mouths, missing limbs, blindness and one specimen that could not be identified as either a dog or a bitch. If the strain was as decrepid as they claimed, how is it so many people wondered longingly where Roy Mee's Gutch-common dogs went to after Roy's unfortunate demise? How is it so many in particular wanted to use Roy's most recent Gutchcommon stud dogs?

The dogs were damned good ones and the world of the real Bedlington is a sadder place for the loss of both Mrs Williamson and Mr Mee. Where success is achieved you will always get this type of criticism. If the Gutchcommon-bred Bedlington does not find favour with everyone is it possibly because when non-Gutchcommon owners see them out working, most stick obediently near to their owners. Hardly spectacular in their enthusiasm possibly, but watch one when a scent is picked up, suddenly the dog becomes alive and excited and in fact I have yet to find one that will false mark quarry to ground, either fox, rabbit or rat. If your Gutchcommon picks up a scent, there's going to be action, and fairly soon at that. When scent is poor or non-existent, a walk with a Gutchcommon may well be forgettable, whereas some terriers may still insist on going to ground for a look or working a hedge bottom.

As a Bedlington to use on a running dog to produce a lurcher, the Gutchcommon Bedlington is ideal and indeed it throws an excellent lurcher, while on this subject I would like to say that I would never use a Bedlington that was not working bred to breed a lurcher. N. Bird, in an article in *Shooting News* in March 1988 spoke of never using anything other than a Rillington-bred Bedlington in creating a Bedlington lurcher and whilst I would certainly agree that an animal bred thus would be ideal in the creation of a lurcher, let me also say that a Gutchcommon stud dog would certainly be of equal excellence, in my view. One person satsified with his Gutchcommon Bedlington lurcher is Bryan Silcox from Newport, Gwent. His Bedlington lurcher Gert is apparently a little treasure according to Bryan and I believe he turned down quite a substantial amount of money for her when she was barely out of puppyhood. Now an adult, this rough-coated blue/black lurcher bitch works the spectrum and her sire was a Gutchcommon-bred dog. According to the late Roy Mee of Leicester his dogs were often used on greyhounds and whippets and in a day and age when Bedlington lurchers are very fashionable I can well believe it.

One of the best known and used of the contemporary Gutchcommon dogs was without doubt Rusty of Gutchcommon and this Bedlington figured in all the recent Gutchcommon pedigrees. Mrs Williamson used him extensively and the pedigree of a Bedlington bred in 1986 shows Rusty of Gutchcommon was used six times in a five-generation pedigree. Rusty of Gutchcommon bred some good pups, none more than the bitch Gutchcommon Russett, the dam of Gutchcommon Rogue, Kentenes Rogue and Rogue of Birkacre, both the last two being owned by Roy Mee.

Roy Mee's outstanding dog Dick, an unregistered dog sired by Gutchcommon Rogue out of Sandy of Gutchcommon was admired by many working Bedlington enthusiasts in recent years. His sire Gutchcommon Rogue was out of Gutchcommon Russett, and therefore the link to Rusty of Gutchcommon was apparent; likewise Sandy of Gutchcommon was by Rusty of Gutchcommon. It is interesting to note that although Rusty was Dick's grandsire and great grandsire on both sides, Argonauts Blue Pierette was an introduction into the strain. This Bedlington bitch was Rusty of Gutchcommon's grandmother, perhaps Mrs Williamson believed in getting value for money from her introductions. Nevertheless, Dick and his litter sister Rustie were very sound Bedlingtons indeed. For some unknown reason both Dick and Rustie were unregistered with the Kennel Club.

A dog called Fletcher owned by Adam Rainsley was out of Rustie by a dog called Sprout. Sprout was sired by Gutchcommon Rogue, brother of Kentenes Rogue and Rogue of Birkacre, both registered dogs. Sprout's mother was Nick Wright's Holly of Thornton, litter sister to Mad Ratter, another registered dog. Fletcher's dam Rustie

Roy Mee's Rusty.

Bedlington bred by Roy Mee and Margaret Williamson.

was also by Gutchcommon Rogue (Sprout and Rustie were half brother and sister); my bet is Sandy of Gutchcommon or her mother in turn, Pella of Gutchcommon, was not registered? The question is, why did Mrs Williamson not register them? I am sure Roy Mee would have preferred them registered as he was against cross-breeding Bedlingtons, but did allow his stud dogs to mate running dogs. Roy valued his registration with the Kennel Club and events proved this to be the case when he tried for many months, unsuccessfully to register or gain the signature to secure the registration of the controversial Roddy.

Quite apart from the much-used Rusty of Gutchcommon, another dog Mrs Margaret Williamson used extensively was Dick of Gutchcommon who was about a quarter Gutchcommon. Dick was bred by Dave Roberts; again this addition to the family Gutchcommon certainly distributed his genetic potential generously. About six times in most five generation pedigrees in most contemporary Gutchcommon dogs. Mrs Williamson's Bedlingtons could be traced quite easily (even the latter-day dogs) all the way back (sometimes through several different lines) to the very beginning of Bedlington history. For this reason and the fact that Margaret maintained basically a good workmanlike terrier, I hope I am not alone in being an admirer of the Gutchcommon dog, as one young lady who recently contacted me said, 'It would be a shame if the Gutchcommon Bedlington died out completely, as this is the type of dog I hope to maintain and work.' This young lady, who apparently used to use her Bedlington for driving rabbits into gate-nets, hopes to keep alive the Gutchcommon type of Bedlington. I for one will watch her progress with interest!

Opposite is a copy of a Bedlington's pedigree and shows just how heavy the Gutchcommon breeding is in most of the dogs used only for work.

Below is the pedigree of Rusty of Gutchcommon bred by and owned by Mrs Margaret Williamson.

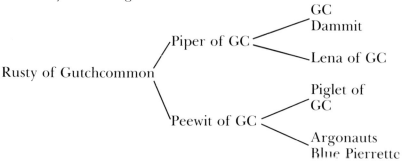

Margaret Williamson

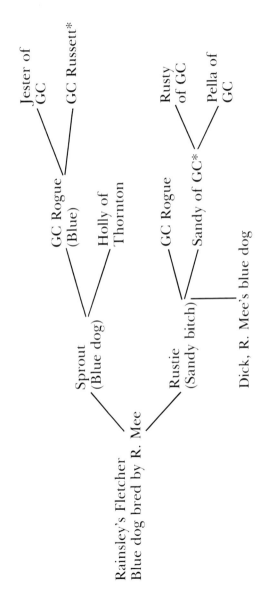

Rainsley's Fletcher
Blue dog bred by R. Mee

Sprout
(Blue dog)

GC Rogue
(Blue)

Jester of
GC

GC Russett*

Holly of
Thornton

Rustie
(Sandy bitch)

GC Rogue

Sandy of GC*

Rusty
of GC

Pella of
GC

Dick, R. Mee's blue dog

* Half sisters both sired by Rusty of Gutchcommon probably one of
the most used of the recent Gutchcommon-bred Bedlingtons.

Roy Mee (who as it were took over from the lady after her death) told many tales of Mrs Williamson's experiences and he used to visit her very regularly. Apparently once he went with her to a hunt show in Wales. Roy said, 'I had clipped and smartened the dogs up, bathed them and thought I would pick up a few prizes.' Mrs Williamson had merely selected a few dogs of her own and loaded them into the back of Roy's vehicle. He said to me, 'I was always surprised how much urine and excreta' (though he did not use those terms), – 'comes out of one of Mrs Williamson's dogs – particularly in the back of my car.' Duly arrived at the show and with dogs entered in and shown Mrs Williamson struggles back to the car with an armful of prizes and her Bedlingtons. 'Where are yours, Roy?' the lady asked. 'Why Mrs Williamson, you've won them all,' he said. Such was the reputation of Mrs Williamson's Gutchcommon dogs around Wales, she undoubtedly cleared up at the working shows.

Mrs Williamson held very strong views and there are tales of her widely publicised condemnation of the show-type Bedlington. Unlike myself, Mrs Williamson thought of Wales as a working Bedlington stronghold and gave several examples of dogs who were working type and were also shown. Her own bitch Pennygraig Lucy from 1933, was bred from a working bitch Lucy, who was also shown. A certain person by the name of Mrs Bruce-Low also bred, it is said, three champions from one individual litter by probably the most famous of all Gutchcommon-bred dogs, Worton Demon.

Like George Newcombe so many years later on, Mrs Williamson gained the dubious distinction of being termed controversial by some. Once, while judging, she put a show champion down to third position, and simply stated that she 'would not be seen dead with any of the respective winners that day' – and this was said to a Cruft's winner. No wonder Mrs Williamson gave up showing just after the war in disgust.

Truly the lady spoke her mind and was well known for her controversial remarks. Like George Newcombe, she believed that poodle blood was used later on especially when showing really started to take off, much in the same way as enthusiasts of other breeds hold similar beliefs; as for example, Fox and Welsh terrier breeding reputedly being in lakelands, etc. Doubtless the more conversant one is with any individual breed the more rumour one will hear to this effect.

Mrs Williamson's pet hate was quite basically the modern show-type Bedlington; like George Newcombe she never considered the type a real or true Bedlington and always considered her dogs the real thing. Mrs Williamson hated faults such as soft, poodle-type coats, and round eyes and ribs, characteristics so often associated with the show dogs.

Although on so many issues Margaret Williamson and George Newcombe agreed with each other, there was however one great dividing line between the two, namely different breeding policies, but it should be pointed out that no bad feelings existed between the two and they always remained on friendly terms. In fact George wrote a really nice letter acknowledging her dedication to the cause of the real Bedlington just after her death. (This letter was published in *Shooting News*.)

In an unsigned article in the Working Type Bedlington Terrier Association's journal, one interesting set of views appeared regarding the Gutchcommon Bedlingtons. It was stated that Gutchcommon dogs of 10 to 20 years ago (late 1960s–70s) were considerably better than the most recently bred dogs. This is something I personally disagree with, as I have found most modern Gutchcommon dogs more than willing to go to ground on fox and to work this quarry enthusiastically and with great determination and drive. I think so many people have failed with Gutchcommon dogs simply because they cannot get on with their natures. People who do understand them are more than complimentary about what is one of the great lines of real Bedlington.

To sum up, I think Mrs Williamson retained type and coat well and, if you are a patient enough person with the right kind of temperament, a Gutchcommon-bred dog might well be your ideal. When Mrs Williamson died a great void was left in the world of the real Bedlington and it will indeed be a hard one to fill, as Margaret was more than an interested party, she was a dedicated and committed person.

The Pedigree of Rogue of Birkacre, owned by Roy Mee

Dick of GC

Pixie of GC

Piglet of GC

Midget of GC

Rusty of GC

Blue Bonnett of GC

Jester of GC

Gutchcommon Russett

Rogue of Birkacre

The Pedigree of Jasper of Kentene (Gutchcommon bred), owned by John Piggin

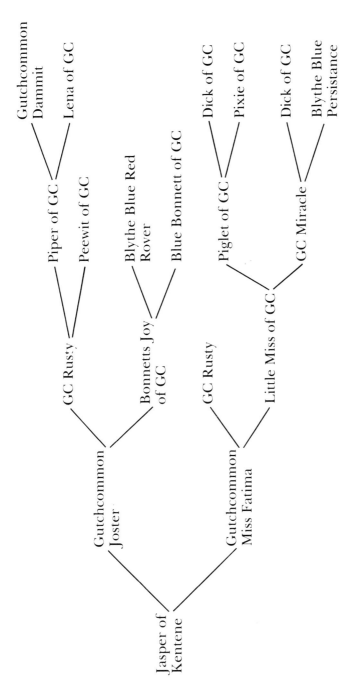

(GC = Gutchcommon)
This Bedlington was actively worked most days with his owner, John Piggin, who is a Council Pest Control Operative.

—6—

Choosing and bringing on a puppy

WHEN LOOKING FOR a good puppy that is likely to be competent at legitimate terrier work, the most obvious starting point will be a scan through various weekly publications, such as *Shooting News* and *Exchange and Mart*; just occasionally one sees Bedlington pups in the *Shooting Times*, though quite rarely nowadays. Now reader, be prepared, all advertisements are not what they may at first appear as the following story will illustrate.

A young fellow wrote to me a short time ago, rather distressed about his Bedlington pup as it was, to quote him, 'Not making the grade.' The pup in question (an 18-month old, young adult would have been more accurate) was liver in colour and a bitch. The following is an extract from his letter. 'I bought a pup a little while ago from a chap who was advertising Bedlington pups for sale; when I rang him up he told me the pups were from good working parents and families, so I asked him if I could go at the weekend and see the pups. He told me never mind the weekend, (he had already sold five of the six pups in the litter) and that it was first come first served, so I told him I wanted one and said I would send a deposit of £20 the next day on the last pup, at which time the chap stopped being a bit stroppy and perked up, in fact he got quite pleasant.'

'When I went at the weekend, the owner of the pups said to me, take your pick mate, which surprised me as I thought I'd got the last pup; when I asked him about this he just said they had all been bought up unseen and the rest were coming the following weekend to pick up their pups. So I picked my pup and went, but she has never ever shown the slightest interest in working, even though I take her out regularly with my brother's border/lakeland who is an excellent ratter, works cover for rabbits and is a demon on a fox. Why is this? Is the Bedlington past it now as a working dog? I've tried everything to get mine going – in a nutshell, it's a load of rubbish, can you please help me?'

Actually this type of letter is not unusual and it is very true that many people start with Bedlingtons, so full, naturally, of hope and ambition, only to be disillusioned with the breed after such an experience. I followed up the information he had given me and contacted the breeder in question and when I rang I told him, 'My friend had a brilliant pup from you,' and 'could you give me details of its sire as I was thinking of using him.' With no prompting at all I got the name, address and telephone number of the owner of the sire and I also obtained the pedigree of the sire from its owner. My young friend had received no written pedigree and was told that 'working-Bedlington people don't keep pedigrees.' (What utter rubbish, though this is often said by those that have something to hide.)

A mere glance at the pedigree told me the sire was 100 per cent show-type bred. Working Bedlington – I think not, working family – definitely not. Now we had to obtain the bitch's pedigree which was not so easy as the con-artist was by now smelling a rat, and in fact, we never did find out how the bitch was bred, although I did see her at a working terrier show with a terribly matted coat and looking generally neglected. Later that day I witnessed the bitch changing hands, an obvious swap, for a rather poor grade looking Staffordshire bull terrier; a few minutes later the dubious character was escorted off the showground, apparently for fighting. Enough said, a person who quite frankly should not be allowed to own a dog, let alone breed pups.

Naturally my young friend learned a lot from this experience and all credit to him for sticking with his, at least half show-type bitch, and although she never did make a good worker, I believe he did breed some rather useful ferreting, and bushing dogs from her when paired to a nice whippet dog. A happy ending this time, but beware this con trick is not pulled on you by an unscrupulous breeder.

So having seen a likely-looking advertisement, which will read something like this: 'Bedlington pups, from working parents, both can be seen, working – pedigrees to be viewed, telephone number, etc.' On the face of it this seems quite promising. When telephoning remember that first impressions are important, not only for yourself, but also for the bona fide breeder who will be taking great steps to ensure his puppies are sold to a good home, so remember your manners for just as you are sussing out him or her, the person on the other end will be sussing out you. More often than not the breeder will invite you to his/her premises, to view the pups. When you get there, the same procedure as buying any other type of dog applies – call the pups to you and watch how nervously or otherwise they approach you. Avoid the nervy ones, pick an adventurous type that shows no signs of a rupture, etc. and make sure you see at least one parent.

But for goodness sake do not make a decision yet. Have you seen the pedigree? Names you will be looking for are Gutchcommon, Rillington, Strike, and Eakring. Any other names will probably (with one exception about to be explained) be show blood, especially where prefixes are used. The exception is a case like Gallants Nomad; no prefix or affix is present, this bitch is all working bred from Rillington parents and this can be easily seen from her pedigree. Similar other instances exist, so do look at the pedigree, that is its real function and it will instantly expose a con artist like the one in the last story. That working Bedlington people do not keep pedigrees is untrue and, I do not know one genuine owner of working-strain Bedlingtons that does not keep authentic pedigrees, and that also includes those who engage in outcrossing programmes; if they do not know the breeding they will tell you so, that's if they have any decency about them.

Assuming everything has gone right and both you and the owner are satisfied, then make your purchase. Things to avoid are: wormy, pot-bellied pups, very young pups under six weeks old, pups that are not strong on their legs and also those that carry excessive white (either feet toes or nails), however you will find most Bedlington pups do carry some white nails and a splash of white on their chests, as do most of the coloured northern terriers; however I do not like excessive white nails, two or three at most, but this is my personal preference. Liver pups at the time you expect to buy them (six to 12 weeks) will be chocolate/brown in colour – blues will be black, at a similar age.

Buying an adult dog

Adult Bedlingtons are just occasionally seen advertised for sale and, like all other adult dogs, can be suspect. On the odd occasions bargains do emerge; it is usually when an enthusiast is selling up and getting out of the game, ill health or pressure from a demanding job, being the usual reasons, but be wary when the latter, as it often means the dog in question has not been socialised and looked after as it should have been.

Be very careful with adult dogs; if the dog is advertised as a working dog as opposed to say, a brood bitch, ask for a trial. Do not under any circumstances, buy anything you consider dodgy; equally so (and this applies also to puppies), if you are satisfied and you have asked the price beforehand, do not try to beat the seller down by haggling. If you have not asked the price by this stage (which most people would have done initially when they 'phoned) and it comes as a shock, say so and bid goodbye. I emphasise, do not haggle, but let the seller come down himself if he wishes. Most good ones however will not, as demand for their excess pups will be high due to their reputation.

Breeding your own puppy
The alternative to buying the correct Bedlington is of course breeding it, which is not as stupid as it first sounds – I can imagine you all saying how can I breed a Bedlington if I have not got one to start with? Very true, though a lot of people entering Bedlingtons do have other types of terrier; for instance you may have a suitable lakeland, border, fell-type terrier, Glen of Imaal or, for the ambitious, a dachshund (the last two will probably cost you more than the Bedlington though). You may feel like breeding your own three-quarter breds, in which case everything said previously applies – check out your bitch's breeding, check out your Bedlington stud dog's breeding, watch out for show-type breeding and you should be alright.

A good, fairly sure-fire way of not getting your fingers burnt is to seek out someone of standing within the Bedlington scene and ask politely if you might correspond with them, telling them you will include a s.a.e. (and do so). However, do not be offended if a person does not always want to correspond, though most will at least reply, even if it's to tell you they will not do so. The reason some people are reluctant to correspond is that it does have its drawbacks as all sorts of lunatics seem to write as well as the genuinely interested. One almost becomes a version of a doggy agony aunt and having experienced these people, I must confess there are times when I do not reply to letters. My pet hates are the time wasters and non-inclusion of a s.a.e. Common sense usually tells you if a person is genuine and is not just trying to secure a day's ratting.

Feeding the puppy
One of the most often-asked questions by the beginner in either Bedlingtons or other breeds is feeding. Since copper retention

Donna with her three liver puppies by Sam.

Three-quarter Bedlington/quarter Glen of Imaal puppies.

reared its head, the Bedlington world has seen everything from old-wives' tales to witch-doctor type advice, on what to feed and not to feed. 'Don't feed that meat it's got too much copper.' 'Don't feed that dog food, it makes their blood too hot.' Most people usually ask at the time they get their first pup, 'What has it been fed on,' or 'What will it eat?' Basically a puppy should get plenty of calcium, essential for building bones and teeth. Many breeders (and I quite frankly loath to use that term breeder as it makes most of them sound like they are in it only for the cash) supplement the calcium found in their ordinary food with puppy meals (specially prepared with extra calcium in it), or cover their pups' food with bone flour.

One of the best breeders of pups I have ever seen is Fred Newman of Leicestershire, one of the few people ever to send Glen of Imaal terriers back to buyers in Ireland. His reputation as a stock man is second to none, even if his method of rearing pups is simplicity itself, albeit, perhaps, a little unorthodox. A pregnant bitch is always fed with green tripe and sheeps heads. She is always allowed access to calves milk (made up from powder) as are all his pups. Finally, as his pups are weaned they go on to minced tripe and it is a well-known fact that Fred Newman's Glen of Imaal terrier pups are always first class. His lurcher pups when he bred those, were of the same quality and I'm sure if he turned his attention to Bedlington terriers his results would be of equal excellence.

Unless you have money to burn I would advise you to stay clear of tinned puppy food and if you want to feed something other than fresh meat I recommend you use one of the dry foods such as Wilsons. These are suitable for puppies as well as adults and are economical. Ask the breeders what they have been feeding the puppy on and to start with stick to this and make any changes gradually, as a puppy's stomach is very delicate and scouring can be potentially fatal.

Inoculation and weaning

At 10–12 weeks get your puppy down to the vet for its injections against distemper, hepatitis, parvovirus, and leptospira jaundice. Despite the cost this is a must for any dog and especially a working terrier that could receive bites from fox and rat. Also make sure it is kept free from worms.

The biggest danger to a puppy of this age is parvovirus and without a doubt this killer virus takes more puppies per year than any other disease. Its arrival is unannounced, its course is swift and in its wake follow many graves. Parvovirus was, since its identification several years ago, the great puppy killer and even today, with our safe, fast, live vaccines, it is still unparalleled in this respect.

My introduction to parvovirus happened at Christmas 1982 – it is one festive season I recollect with dread and deep regret. The week prior to Christmas had been a particularly hectic one as I had just moved house and I promised myself that immediately after the holiday season was over I would inoculate the lurcher pups we had. The pups, all bitches, were well when I moved house and had been kept at the new house within a brick shed (to keep them isolated until I had got them inoculated). One particular bitch, a little red pup, had established herself top of the pecking order and the other two were never allowed to lie up on her bed – which was, funnily, a wheelbarrow full of straw. This bitch loved lying here and woe betide the pup brave enough to claim it.

Christmas 1982 was one of those years I believe when we got a Sunday on 26 December instead of Boxing Day and about eight a.m. on this day I went into the building to check on the pups. This morning only two of the pups bounded up to greet me when I opened·the shed door and, rather surprisingly, the dominant red bitch pup lay obviously distressed in the wheelbarrow. Examination revealed the straw fouled with bloody excreta and the pup unable to stand. Its body, like the straw, was equally fouled and the characteristic sickly-sweet stench I will never forget and always associate with parvovirus. A half-hour later found me at the vet's and my worst fears were confirmed, parvovirus was the cause of the pup's obvious critical problem and she was put to sleep immediately.

The two remaining pups were apparently unaffected, though I did not need the vet's warning that these two pups would in all probability succumb to this, the most horrible of the canine diseases. A live parvovirus jab was administered and we would just have to wait and see what card fate would deal. Sure enough, on the following Wednesday both the other pups were stricken down by the virus; the vet said it was unlikely either would survive the night, and in less than the space of a week, three apparently healthy pups had been reduced to dehydrating, bleeding, dying wrecks as the killer disease caused the walls of their intestines to cave away and be passed as bloody excreta. 'It's in the lap of the Gods,' the vet had said; he hardly instilled hope in me and, quite frankly, as I put in yet more clean straw and adjusted the heat lamp to its correct position, I gave the pups no chance whatsoever. My worst fears were confirmed next morning when I saw a little blue bitch dead, two down, one to go.

All Thursday and Friday the last bitch held on. Vanadine diluted in boiled water with sugar in it and left to cool, was poured down the pup's throat every four hours, and although more went on the bedding, myself and the pup's fur rather than down its throat, it did succeed in stopping the animal from dehydrating. Friday, New Year's Eve, and I was left with one pup; six days of parvovirus and I felt drained emotionally and physically. 'It ain't gonna make it,' I told my wife, 'That's it, it's going to die.' I had given up; however, I had not reckoned on the pup's resilience.

New Year's Eve, and I had bought tickets for a New Year ball several weeks before Christmas. 'I'm not going,' I told my wife. 'The break away from the pups will do you good,' my wife replied. 'There's nothing you can do now, leave a bowl of steamed fish down for her – You have done all you can – let's go!' My wife's suggestion had more than a hint of appeal as well as good sense about it; I was tempted, and ultimately went to the ball. At three a.m. on the first of January, I approached the shed door and I could hear a whimpering within; I flung open the door, and the last pup lay there, and lifted her head and wagged her tail feebly, the blood had stopped, the smell had gone and the bowl of fish had been half eaten. Now it was parvovirus's turn to die, this pup had beaten it – what a way to ring in the New Year!

I gave the pup away to my father after everyone had told me she'd be no good for working. 'She'll die after twelve months from heart failure,' 'her stamina will be poor,' 'it will be rubbish for work,' were all comments that were made. However they were all wrong, although my dad keeps her as a pet and house dog, over the years she has worked successfully, hare, rabbit and fox and even bred her own litter of pups – so much for the bad heart!

Nevertheless, heart damage does manifest itself in apparently recovered parvo victims, basically it seems to come down to just when the puppy falls victim to parvovirus. Vets will tell you heart damage is only experienced as a result of parvovirus when the heart is developing in the early weeks of life. Possibly it was that my dad's lurcher had passed that stage and as a consequence fortunately never experienced heart problems.

Recently a friend of mine said the only thing to do with a parvovirus victim is to have it put to sleep, 'because it will be no good if it recovers.' I know what he means; however, I do have to disagree with him especially in the light of the lurcher bitch my father has, but then again, I am a little biased here! My experience with parvovirus proves that you do not have to take a pup uninoculated on a lead, to contract parvovirus; visitors feet, clothes, etc. will all carry the virus into your premises. Disinfectants help and of course should be used – Jeyes Fluid used with boiling water will kill most of the bugs, sheep dip and many miscellaneous detergents will all be found satisfactory and should be used.

Nevertheless, you will always get those who begrudge paying the vet to inoculate a pup. My friends Adrian and Sophie had two friends who fell neatly into this category. The couple in question came into the world of field sports with a bang, believe me – the brand new wax jacket, moleskin trousers, Hunter green wellington boots, not to forget the checked shirt, tie and cap. They really wanted to look the part, wanted to attend coursing meets, go out with the hunt, buy a hip flask and generally talk 'plum in the gob' as they say in Liverpool.

When the couple found out that Adrian and Sophie had a ferreting friend, they immediately got themselves introduced to me and wanted to get a terrier. 'I haven't got any,' I told them, 'but I'll give you a couple of addresses where you might get fixed up.' Eventually, they got yet another address from one of the people I had put them in touch with, and by coincidence they bought a very poor-grade Bedlington. Mind you, it was the bees knees brilliant, the best – as it happened they had been ripped off and when I saw it I told them to take it back. No-way, this dog was a world beater and off they went complete with wax-jackets and duff dog to do the rounds of the country shows.

Twelve months came and went and Adrian often told me about his two friends who by now had got a lurcher as well, another good 'un and mind, best bloodlines to boot. 'It's coursing foxes well,' Adrian repeated what he had been told, 'Good,' I said, 'I'm glad.' A couple of months went by and I was at a hunt show (a rare occurrence for me) and there were Adrian and Soph's friends, still dressed like they were in a competition for yuppy of the year, so I walked over. 'Y'er alright?' I said to yuppy number one, 'Oh, delighted to make your acquaintance again, how are you?' There was no doubt about it, they had really got that toff imitation off to a tee. A group of hunt supporters were gathered around the yuppies; they all knew them and it was all very civilised.

'How's your lurcher,' I said, 'still coursing the foxes well?' Number one yuppy's face went through shades of purple to scarlet, all the hunt servants turned their heads and muttered. 'I don't course foxes, young man,' said the embarrassed yuppy; I knew the cause for his embarrassment, but did not quite like the way he gave

Aged 10 weeks.

Bedlington puppy.

me 50 good reasons why no one should course foxes, even in non-hunt country (that is to say on land that no hunt rides across). I explained that in urban areas and non-hunt country it was legitimate practice and many lurcher men are often called out to deal humanely with problem foxes. He would not have it, which I could probably understand, had he not bragged to Adrian about his lurcher's prowess at stopping foxes. In a relatively short time the yuppies had progressed from being green beginners to being instant experts and I quite forgot after that point about the two, their lurcher and their little Bedlington.

What has this to do with parvovirus? I hear you ask. Well, hold on a little – it's all about to unfold. Adrian and Sophie had bought a nice little border terrier bitch (as an adult), the dog thought the world of them and they felt the same way about her. 'Let's have some puppies with her, Adrian,' Sophie had said, so when the bitch came into season she was paired to a nice black terrier dog. Three days after the pups were born, I was at Adrian's place to dock the pups tails, when who should arrive on their way home from visiting a terrier enthusiast, but the two yuppies. Out came their Bedlington, closely followed by three pups (two bitches and a dog) and all about as poor as the dam.

As usual, Adrian's pups were looked over, the docking criticised, and then the bragging started. 'We have had the litter because so many people have told us they want a pup from us.' I went to speak but, as my mouth opened, I was cut short. 'Are you looking for a puppy?' sniffed the yuppy glancing sideways at me. 'No,' I replied, 'Though if I was I might have one of Adrian's pups,' pointing at the border cross pups. 'Oh, you don't want one of those; have a Bedlington terrier off me. I'll do you one for £200.' I could not stifle my amusement, and as I walked away and got into my car, I bet they could hear me laughing as I started the engine and drove away!

About three weeks after this I visited Adrian again. I told him that Joe, the terrier man the yuppies had recently visited had just lost a complete litter of Russell-type pups to parvovirus. 'Did he really? You know the two yuppies, they lost two pups as well; the only one to survive was the one they had got inoculated.' We worked out that the two yuppies had taken the disease to Joe's and as a direct result, he had lost his litter of Russells. 'I hope my pups will be alright,' said Adrian. I reassured him, 'Probably they will be Adrian, at three days old the bitch's colestrum would protect them with any luck.' Adrian did have luck on his side, as all his pups survived.

Parvovirus carries off pups so fast it is unbelievable; one day a dog can be well, or probably a little off colour, the next day it is dead. I remember seeing a nice collie-bred lurcher with a wall eye, well one day, dead and buried the next. In concluding on parvovirus, do not learn the hard way, get your puppy immunised by your vet and see that you do it!

Training
I include in this, socialising, of which the puppy should have plenty. Make sure that he is played with as much as possible and not just left in his kennel with no human contact. This is a part of the puppy's development where children can be very useful.

Different people train dogs in different ways according to the type of work for which they wish to use their dog. One young man from Liverpool I spoke to recently seemed particularly concerned about getting a dog to go into water. When I told him Bedlingtons will work in water, he replied that he was more bothered about the dog retrieving a ball out of the canal if he threw one in for it, and asked if they would do this. My reply was, 'I do not know many terriers who will chase a ball at all; however, I know plenty who will work quarry in water.'

It is not normally recessary to train a dog to the level of perfection that we are used to seeing in an obedience ring at Crufts. But the basic commands should be taught. In a working dog I like the animal to come when it is told to and to sit still or to stay when it is told to. If I want a dog to stay close when quarry is possibly near rather than hunting up, I want it to respond to close, but not heeling (think about it). So many people want their so-called working dogs to perform some weird old circus tricks. I knew one Bedlington enthusiast who, upon arriving at anyone's house, always asked where the nearest stretch of water was. His excuses were many – 'the dog is hot and likes a dip,' or 'it wants a drink' – all sorts of silly little excuses, which basically translated meant, 'I want to do my party piece with the dog' – which was no more than throwing a stick in the water for it to fetch.

Training by my definition also means breaking pups to livestock, ferrets, etc. This can be achieved by getting a pup out early and among animals larger than himself, which at a couple of months old is usually just about everything (sheer height seems to frighten most pups). Should a pup be brave enough to lunge at forbidden animals (on a lead I might add), reprimand him straightaway in a sharp stern voice, saying 'No' or giving him a light tap; I emphasize a light tap, do not beat the dog up like some of the five-minute-wonder boys suggest. I write this with a twinge in my heart for, only last night, the best ferret I ever owned died at the jaws of an unbroken lakeland terrier, apparently as keen to kill ferrets as rats.

A puppy that will not respond to a 'come' command is quite frankly a liability. Not only will it get used to hunting up on its own, flushing game and vermin, but the bolting quarry will often be pushed out too far away for effective interception by lurchers, other dogs or guns. Once into this habit a dog is often impossible to break of it and one consequence is that a fox is put to ground in an unlocated earth.

As I have said, a dog once in this habit is often impossible to break of it and also, once it is adult, subsequent pups will learn from its example. Sometimes this type of behaviour is hereditary and the pup comes from a line that behaves in this way and quite obviously it is worth asking any breeder about. (Whether he/she will be honest enough to answer truthfully is another matter.) Another aspect to this problem is dogs that behave in this way frequently get into trouble (or your dog will get the blame if any damage has been done) and anyone who owns such a dog is in for a very worrying time. Whether we like it or not, cats are regarded by many Bedlingtons as fair game (the sight of one is often enough to turn 90% of Bedlingtons into raging demons. It is not only cats that one has to beware of in the countryside either. What happens if a dog enters a badger sett? Believe me, an owner could quite easily find himself in court being given a hefty fine if this occurs.

Quite obviously then, for all these reasons, a Bedlington that displays an air of keenness about it, should have that keenness directed into the correct channels. The all-important part of obedience in any breed of terrier is responding immediately to a call to come back to its owner, and keeping close, not only because of the danger of owning an unresponsive dog but also because it is very important in effective hunting. Particularly from the lurcher or gun man's point of view and in these days when lurchers and lurcher men are more and more involved with Bedlingtons, I am sure this is a matter many will consider as one worthy of paramount consideration.

Get your puppy out young, let him play, let him socialise and give the pup all the love and attention he deserves; after all your pup is with you, or should be, if all goes well, for the rest of his life. Feed him well and keep him free from worms, teach him basic obedience, sit, lie, stay, come; all of these will be learnt easily by most puppies, if the time is put in by you. Look after him now and his treasure will unfold and gladden your heart, just as he will surely break it when his time is done (the ones who break your heart are always the best). Make no mistake you want the best. One day in winter his time will come to prove his true worth.

—7—

Managing and Keeping the Working Bedlington

OBVIOUSLY, IF A BEDLINGTON is your only dog then problems in kennelling are on the whole minor. Most first-time Bedlington owners who intend to keep only one dog, generally state from the outset that they intend to keep it indoors, and for several reasons the Bedlington terrier is an ideal choice for a house-dog; namely: it never drops hair; like most terriers is a good little guard dog; it is not that big that it is forever in the way.

Kennelling

However a lot of working terrier and lurcher enthusiasts nowadays do not fall into this one-dog-in-the-house category; a majority are multiple dog keepers and it is here I feel that many problems occur in the kennelling of a Bedlington.

Ideally one dog per kennel and run is the foolproof way of minimising, if not completely wiping out the potential problem of kennel-fighting. However, it is not everyone who can take this precaution. Right from the beginning, let me state that Bedlingtons will kennel together. The golden rule is to kennel only two terriers together, and then only two bitches (there is an exception to this however, which I will explain presently) or one dog and one bitch.

Three terriers together, whether all bitches, or one dog and two bitches, or sin-of-sins, more than three Bedlingtons, is just begging for trouble and is, believe me, the proverbial time-bomb quietly ticking away and just waiting to explode – and explode it invariably will, in a barrage of blood, gore and tremendous heartache, not to mention expense in the form of vets' fees. Surely nobody would be so foolish as to kennel three terriers together, especially game

80

terriers like working Bedlingtons? 'No,' I hear you say, but I can recall seeing four terriers together and one of these dogs was a hard Stafford/lakeland, another was a smooth-coated black fell type bitch, a third was a four-month-old bitch pup bred from these two, and a fourth an impeccably working-bred Bedlington bitch pup similarly aged to the last pup. Just for good measure picture a mid-winter scene where the dogs are fed but not exercised, at approximately 6 pm and never again do they see the outside world from their shed prison until 24 hours later.

What, reader, is your reaction to this scene? I hope most sincerely it is one of amazement that surely no one could be so naive as to attempt to keep game dogs together like this for practically 24 hourly periods and not expect problems of the worst bloody type occurring. Perhaps such a terrier keeper is a novice and if this is the case perhaps we could forgive him, when the inevitable finally happened. Did this person fall into this category? The fact is the said terrier keeper did not fall conveniently into this slot at all and was a terrier owner of some years standing and, to use his own word, 'experienced'.

One evening at 6 pm, his torch illuminated the draughty, dark wooden shed, its earth floor pitted with long-ago-dug craters and not-so-old ones, to relieve the imprisoned terriers' boredom. The stench of dog urine was more acute tonight for some reason or other, and where was that other pup? The blue Bedlington pup was bounding about his heels as usual but, mind you, that Stafford/lakeland and the black fell bitch looked a bit sheepish over there on their wooden benches, moving their heads owl like in the torch's beam. As he stood there for a second taking in the situation, a whimpering alerted him to a dark corner of the shed, where the Stafford/lakeland cross fell bitch pup was behind a few sheets of corrugated roofing. He picked it up and took it back into the house; the pup on examination of its throat revealed bite marks and miscellaneous cuts to its face. A subsequent visit to the vet's meant the remaining three terriers would have to wait a few hours longer until they received their daily meal.

Cursing that little Bedlington pup for trying to take the throat out of his pup, that was now temporarily safe and sound within the confines of the veterinary surgeon's premises where it would spend at least a few nights to recover from its ordeal. It's that damn pup, he had told the vet – what's worse, the vet never questioned his statement!

Three days had passed and he had quite forgotten about his killer Bedlington while he toiled away at his factory job;

nevertheless, tonight he would get his pup back from the vet's (and the bill) and all would be well, or so he hoped. He decided to feed the dogs before he went to the vet's, however and to his great surprise, the Bedlington was not its normal self. No bounding up to its master to jump up those oily overalls; no, instead it slunk out from underneath those corrugated sheets, 'Gave you a smack have they?' he spluttered, thinking the pup had tried to cause trouble with the two adult terriers, 'Serves you right,' he mumbled and fed the dogs and went off to the vet's to get the Bedlington pup's victim from the other night.

He duly collected his pup, took her home and, wait for it, put her back in with her parents and the killer Bedlington! How he did not hear (or at least his neighbours) the adult terriers as they slew the hybrid terrier and Bedlington pup that night is beyond me. However, kill them they did, as he tearfully told me, the hybrid pup's throat was ripped out and the Bedlington was practically torn in half. I know this kind of situation is predictable, and just how he had not seen it coming off, is absolutely beyond me, nevertheless, this unfortunate episode happened, proving beyond any doubt that terriers should be kept separately, preferably, or only in pairs. I have one thing to add to the 'pair' theme – do not ever keep two dogs (males) together.

Keeping two dogs (males) together except in very extreme cases is quite simply asking for trouble, as one is always dominant to the other. Particularly in game dogs' cases, the chances of one backing off even when it is getting the worst of the punishment is extremely unlikely, and certainly far less than it is in the cases of more passive breeds – Bedlington terriers do not generally fall into the latter category. For this reason particularly, game bitches who do not suffer fools gladly (which usually means young adults) should be watched no matter what they are kennelled with. Generally speaking, if a pair of terriers are brought up together from puppy-hood, then no long-term problems seem to be encountered; however, should a fight occur, take heed of your warning and for goodness' sake, separate those two terriers as next time you may not be on hand.

In contemplating keeping two dogs together, let commonsense prevail. Never ever be tempted to keep three dogs or more together. Both Mrs Margaret Williamson of the Gutchcommon strain and George Newcombe of North Yorks have kept terriers in numbers, but have only ever kennelled two dogs together.

Bedlingtons are tough little terriers and this stands them in good stead when an individual decides to keep it, or them, outside in a

Anyone at home?

J. Piggin's Sable returning from ground.

kennel and run. Keeping Bedlingtons in sheds is fine as long as you are in the position to take the dog out for a few hours' walk daily. Quite simply, it is cruel to expect a dog to stay shut up for many hours, not to mention the mess it will make.

Runs should be concrete or slabbed with a good base and of course have good drainage. Now beware, dog-runs attract rats, even if you own demon little ratting terriers and, make no mistake, if rats are in the vicinity they will be attracted to dog runs as surely as they are to chicken pens. A friend of mine who keeps lurchers is always telling me he has found yet another dead or half-eaten rat on his dog run floor. Despite the fact that some of his resident rat colony gets taken occasionally by one of his lurchers and he traps them regularly enough as well, still the rats come.

Eventually, when enough is enough, he ferrets out the rats. However, only a matter of weeks elapse before another colony of rats moves in, reopening all the old exits and entry holes. Basically, the solution to his problem is a simple one, if somewhat tedious and laborious. The whole run needs to come up and a concrete one laying. A good two feet of hardcore below the level of the ground with six inches of concrete above, a slight angle going to the centre of the run, with a gully for drainage, Thus a practical, rat-free run can be obtained.

Different people require varying types of run and there is quite a number of good commercially produced ones on the market, ranging through wood to metal frames. Many people are quite capable of building their own, whilst less practical folk have a skilled friend or know a friendly carpenter, who will oblige for a decent price. A robust type of wire will just about complete any run (preferably galvanised) and a good, draught-free, dry, raised kennel will be the only other requirement an individual will need for a secure, adequate run.

Many people nowadays use shredded waste paper for their dogs to lie upon, and very adequate it is too. I might add that enthusiasts of white-bodied dogs often fight shy of using shredded newspaper as the black printer's ink sometimes comes off the paper and on to the dogs. Nevertheless, paper does have the benefit of being easy to dispose of (burning) and is a cheap, safe, type of bedding for working dogs. Traditional bedding materials such as hay and straw are often hazardous and certainly should never be used for whelping litters of pups. Husks, seeds and all manner of foreign material can often be found in such bedding. Given a choice, I would almost certainly use hay in preference to straw. Even so, grass-seed heads can often get into eyes and behind the eye itself.

Let me assure you, reader, it is not pleasant for the onlooker, let alone the stricken animal.

Conclusion to bedding – plenty of shredded waste paper everytime – hay as a standby.

Maintaining the coat

Whatever way you decide you are going to house your Bedlington, one thing will be uppermost in your mind. How am I going to maintain that coat? To be perfectly honest a lot of working enthusiasts do not maintain it. The macho-men are usually the worst in this respect (haven't we all met them), the 'I'm not gonna ponce my dog up like a show dog' type of routine. The fact is, nobody ever suggests that they do. However, all hirsute or hairy dogs do need a good haircut from time to time. Not only does such a practice improve the coat's appearance but all the newly grown hair appears cleaner, crisper and better in texture and colour. Now, never once would I suggest that you have your dog cut in a show trim, throat trimming (where hair should be longer in a working dog, not shorter) is not advisable. Neither is an accentuated top-knot or profuse leg furnishings. These are all the things the stylists (of which there are now many) will leave your terrier with.

Initially most people usually do get their Bedlington cut by one of the mobile dog beauticians that we are so accustomed to seeing in nigh on every pet shop window or newspaper advertisement. The events that follow are usually in this order: The hairdresser arrives at your house and is introduced to the Bedlington pup; the pet beautician will insist on the owner being called the dog's mummy or daddy – these pet beauticians have some funny ideas. You will then be told 'A Bedlington, you don't see many of these, in fact this is the first I've seen'. There is worse to come. 'I'll look the breed up in my little book'. Out will come a pocket book guide to all dogs and on the page with the Bedlington, will be a photograpgh of a classic off-white show Bedlington, complete with show cut. An hour's snipping will transform your blue/black or chocolate ball of wool into a punk rocker look-alike that little children (and some bigger ones) will point their fingers at and fall about in fits of laughter.

But what really are the alternatives? Cut it yourself. At this point I hear you say (well at least some of you), 'I have not got the patience to do that type of thing'. Rubbish, I say, because if you are a man and you have the patience to shave you can cut a Bedlington. If you are a woman and you can comb your hair, you can cut a

A good all round working Bedlington/lakeland.

Ratting with (top) a Bedlington cross-bred and (bottom) a pure-bred.

Bedlington! This is my own way – other people may well do it differently. I like a Bedlington's body coat (back, brisket) to be around half an inch in length, this is enough to protect its skin from briars, etc. when hunting rabbits in thick cover. Alternatively, it's not that long that it collects terrific amounts of soil, clay, etc. when working below ground to fox. If you cut the body coat at around the suggested half-inch length this should suffice.

Try to cut following the general body shape of the terrier. The neck and throat of a Bedlington should preferably be a little shorter (for appearance) at about quarter of an inch, though not the almost shaved effect the show people use. You can leave a top-knot, if you wish, not too long or profuse as this leaves the dog at an obvious disadvantage when it attempts to enter rough-cover and can be extremely off-putting for a puppy just starting to hunt cover. Most head studies of Bedlingtons depict the dog with as little atop as possible which, in many cases, is achieved by trimming, leaving muzzle hair in a line corresponding accordingly to the occiput of the head; in fact, I like it cut this way myself.

However, the old-type dogs' heads were not cut this way – from the nose to the eyes the dog's fur was cut short to the skin, leaving a very different shape to a head study than is seen normally today. There is absolutely no reason in the world why you should not cut a dog's head fur this way, if you so desire. Dogs' appearances in those early days were so different and really do justify the saying 'as different as chalk and cheese' when compared with their modern-day counterparts. Not only were Bedlingtons' heads cut differently, their coat style was different and Bedlingtons had their coats plucked into style and not cut, which strengthens suggestions that Bedlington coats in those far-off days were not of todays abysmal show-ilk, so very poor and soft.

As with the body of the Bedlington, follow its head shape when trimming. Allow the extra for the top-knot length, to set off a top-knot. Make sure the hair length lifts suddenly from the base of the skull where it joins the neck (it will be set off because the neck hair will be shorter here). Cut the hair shorter on the bottom jaw and underneath its eyes, leaving the sides of the muzzle (top-jaw) with hair corresponding to the top-knot's length. As for the Bedlington's ears, again follow the overall shape, being extremely careful not to snip the ear (anyone who is familiar with working terriers will know just how much ears bleed from even the smallest nick). Many people leave the traditional Bedlington feather ear tips, again a matter to be decided by yourself. I do like to see ear tips feathered, as this is in keeping with the original dogs, though I do

87

not like to see it over emphasised and of a silly proportion as is seen in many modern-day show dogs.

Regarding leg furnishings, perhaps it is better to refer to it as long leg fur – cut it all off and leave around a quarter-inch length. A point to remember is that many of the Gutchcommon strain of Bedlington do not grow much in the way of leg furnishings, which is in retrospect quite fortunate. The tail of a Bedlington should be cut short along its length and be whip like. The true old-fashioned dogs used to have a feathered underside, though I feel this is relatively insignificant nowadays. For hygiene reasons, it is advisable for the dog to have short, manageable fur around the base of the dog's tail, particularly the underside.

Ear plucking

Combing or regular brushing is about all that one needs to do to a Bedlington, plus one other thing which is important and that is – ear plucking. Bedlington terriers, like all full dropped eared dogs, are very susceptible to ear disorders which is usually referred to in the broadest terms as canker. Most ear cases referred to popularly as canker are caused by a mite, while others are caused by a build up of wax and debris within the ear channel; it is the latter type that is usually encountered in Bedlington terriers. The fact is, it can often be overcome by plucking the dog's ears. This basically means pulling hairs from down the channel of the ear with your fingers (those you can reach) and with blunt, clean tweezers those you cannot. Puppies, although at pains to try and convince you this is not essential, should be subjected to this practice from an early age. Failure to do so will almost invariably result in so-called canker sooner or later. All hair within the ear channel will need to be plucked away. Watch out particularly for hair from this vicinity that has a red waxy substance adhered to it, as this is a sure sign that canker will manifest itself should this warning be disregarded.

What, then, should one do if the dog becomes infected with canker? Fortunately there are some good ear cleansers readily available straight off the chemist's shelf. Boots, the chemist chain, do an extremely good one, another is 'Leo's' and several other similar brands exist, all of which seem to keep canker at bay. However, the old saying 'prevention is better than cure' is very true and that preventative cure is ear plucking. One should be aware that if the canker is caused by a mite, it is contagious and will probably affect all your dogs. Seek veterinary advice if in doubt, and of course if your actions are not doing any good (i.e. ear cleansers), again, consult your vet. Believe me, your dog will leave you in no doubt that he has canker in one form or another, for he will scratch and scratch at his ears. He will rub his head against anything convenient – wire runs, the interior of kennels, your leg, anything. This scratching will be prolonged, savage and ferocious. The dog will shake his head repeatedly and temporary or partial deafness often accompanies such symptoms.

Canker, either wet or dry, contagious or not, is serious. Dogs affected are miserable, not to mention uncomfortable. In the severe cases, cauliflower ears like those of a boxer are often encountered, and the ear is usually always hot. Lotions and ear cleansers will keep canker at bay, but as I have said, prevention is better than cure and ear-plucked dogs rarely suffer from ear disorders. Once I saw a canker cured quite by accident. Some chicken bones had accidentally been eaten and one of the bone fragments had lodged in the dog's jaw and was making its exit via its eye. Naturally the vet performed an operation to help save the dog's sight in this eye and to his credit succeeded in doing so. A course of antibiotics to combat any possible infection was prescribed by the vet and low and behold, the dog's ear which had always been affected by canker spewed forth a goo of mess and matter. The ear dried up and never again did the problem recur, – a nice ending. Make no mistake, however, canker is anything but nice.

Feeding

As far as I'm concerned, flesh-based diets take some beating, as the dog is basically a carnivore. However, dry foods nowadays are excellent and very good to use when flesh is scarce, or perhaps in hot weather when fresh meat attracts blowflies in their thousands. Of the dry foods on the market there are many and, basically, it's take your choice. Such complete dry foods can be fed with just boiling water added or preferably with minced meat (I prefer tripe personally), at the end of the day – it's your choice, however. If you can get hold of sheeps' heads (sometimes because of public health regulations this can be difficult) or fresh green tripes, then I do not envisage a person's dogs suffering as a result of their diets. Bedlingtons are no different from any other dog really, so if you already have a lurcher or another terrier that's healthy, I certainly don't envisage your Bedlington suffering from being fed similarly.

Just as ferrets thrive on flesh, likewise do dogs – therefore my advice is where possible feed naturally, feed flesh.

Keen and raring to go.

Exercise
In writing a chapter that I hope will serve as a basic guideline to keeping a Bedlington terrier healthy and fit, I feel it is also worth

mentioning road-work and sadly this is one area that is overlooked by many. Road-work builds and strengthens muscle, just as it does in any athlete and make no mistake, that is what a working dog is – an athlete with one purpose in life, performance whose genetic potential will be passed on to the next generation with any luck.

So many people seem to think that working and running their dogs across fields is sufficient to keep them fit and whilst I would agree it certainly does so, road work is still important. Walking dogs at a pace on a short lead on roads is excellent for getting them fit and keeping them in peak condition, especially in the summer months when a hunter or huntress might not be using fields to exercise the ward or wards. I will say nothing on distance, except, use your own judgement and discretion. Obviously not just once round the block, but it need not be a marathon hike either. Both dog and human will benefit from this practice.

—8—

Ailments

THE AILMENTS THAT affect the Bedlington terrier are the same as for other breeds of dog with one exception, copper toxicosis. Copper toxicosis, although reputed to be found in other breeds has, as far as I know, been diagnosed only in Bedlingtons.

Accidents can happen to anyone of course, while some are unavoidable others are down to appalling stockmanship and could quite easily be avoided. A tragic accident that happened to me once involved a Bedlington terrier and my old beloved Blue a terrific working lurcher, whose loyalty to me was unsurpassed and whose jealousy would have put the proverbial scorned woman to shame. So jealous was Blue of any dog, if I ever even spoke to one let alone patted one on the head, that I used to have to be extremely careful, especially where pups were concerned. My Jack Russell bitch knew this and stayed well clear of Bluey as she wandered around the place surveying her domain with an air of arrogance.

No matter what, Blue would always greet any new dog (even friends) with a little bit of B.B.Y.U. which stands basically for 'Blue beats you up', when she found the opportune moment.

Usually the skirmishes looked far worse than they really were. Blue would never even look at the proposed victim, not a growl or murmour would erupt from her throat. No raised hackles or the slightest indication of an imminent attack were to be seen, in fact Blue would draw you into a false sense of security by even playing with the pup. The bottom line was never trust Blue with a smaller dog, weaker or younger than she was, else rest assured she would have it. Couple this with the mistake of making a fuss of the dog, and you had the recipe for a sure spot of puppy bashing from Blue.

On every occassion that Blue had attacked another animal that she saw as a potential threat to her supremacy and her position as my number one dog, she would bowl the pup on to its back, mouth its neck and stand over it in a posture of triumph. With Bess, my little blue Bedlington pup, it was quite different, we had made the mistake of fussing Bessy from the word go. Everywhere I went the pup went, perhaps foolishly I allowed her total liberty, even to the point that she sat on the chairs in the house, which Blue was never allowed to do. One Saturday, I had come home from shopping and went outside the back door to check something or other while Bess followed me like a shadow as usual. Blue saw her chance and struck. The puppy was perhaps two feet from my heel, and in the time it takes for one to turn round Blue had attacked the pup and backed off a few feet. The pup, squealing madly, was spinning round in circles. I picked her up and from the angle of her jaws it was obvious they were smashed. A subsequent visit to the vet's revealed no less than fifteen fractures to both jaws and Bess had to be destroyed.

Both Bedlingtons and Bedlington lurchers are decidedly jealous dogs. In some individuals it is worth remembering this; although jealousy is not an ailment, I feel it does (as on this occassion) precede tragic consequences. In some cases, preventive action is needed, for instance, never trust a jealous dog with puppies. Quite apart from her jealous actions, Blue never displayed any aggression while working with other dogs, except, perhaps, if another dog sniffed any of the quarry that I had handled.

Fits and convulsions

Any dog can suffer from fits or convulsions and a whole range of things can bring on attacks. Some are epileptic, others not. Either way, a dog having a fit or convulsion is not a pretty sight. Fits on the whole are fairly rare in Bedlington's but they do happen nevertheless. If you have never seen a dog suffering from a fit you are lucky and I hope you never do. However, perhaps it is best I describe to you what actually happens, just in case it does happen and you will then know the procedure to follow. I speak again from bitter experience.

A dog of any age (though most do seem to be elderly) can seem perfectly healthy and as right as rain, and then will become distressed, moaning and whimpering and at this point it usually loses balance and falls over. The convulsion has started. Now you will be needed and you will need to be calm and positive. Spasms will wrack the dogs body, its neck will arch back, the eyes will roll backwards, and the jaws will champ and froth. The stricken animal will thrash about. Your job is to stop that happening, so hold the dog as still as you can. Keep the dog held and try to pull the animals neck down nearer to its chest, personal experience has proved to me that this helps, when an attack is happening. These attacks are often only a couple of minutes in length or up to five perhaps. Longer periods involving an attack are usually a series of fits happening immediately one after each other.

The causes for these fits can be multiple, epilepsy (and just like humans there is medication) or an oncoming illness, which is often a serious one like heart problems. Diet can be the cause and some highly strung animals, always so very nervous and edgy, can be susceptible to convulsions. A veterinary surgeon is your next stop after the dog has recovered and this recovery time can vary greatly. The dog will need to be kept very quiet and still, preferably in a dark room and offer the affected animal a drink – it will often be parched. After a while the dog will want to get up, so let it, but keep a very careful watch and remember another fit can happen at any time. Your vet will carry out tests to determine whether it is epilepsy or not and it will be up to him and yourself whether you want your dog to live with that. Your vet will probably question you on your dog's diet and may well advise you to change it if he decides it is not helping in your dog's recovery or indeed that it is contributing to its present problem.

On the other hand the conditions may well be worse than that; unfortunately, dogs with heart-related problems usually suffer firstly from fits before any other symptoms of heart disease start to manifest themselves. The heart with a murmur (an erratic beat) is not pumping blood properly, and the brain denied a proper blood flow can often result in fits, followed by partial blindness. Worse still if not enough blood is being sent to the liver, this dysfunctions causing toxins and water to be retained in the body. The end result is a bloated gut, known more commonly as dropsy. A dog suffering this will be treated with diuretic tablets to make it urinate; some respond, others do not. If not, death is inevitable. The liver has gone, the dog will bloat, its appetite will gradually get less while its thirst will be greatly increased. As a consequence the dropsy will get more severe. Have the dog put to sleep!

Poisonous plants
If you have ever had a puppy or bred a litter, you will no doubt be aware that they are forever getting into mischief; it is part of life and indeed essential training for the future and nowhere is that more important than in working dogs. All pups chew harmless

little things, generally carpets, shoes and slippers and other non-poisonous items. (Mind you, thinking of the state of some of the feet I have seen go into slippers, I'm not so sure.) Nobody ever tells pups to leave alone poisonous plants, in fact some positively like them, and sadly some die from doing so.

One terrier pup I knew of that had just had its inoculations, apparently contracted that greatest puppy killer, parvovirus. I saw the pup and it certainly did not have parvovirus (once seen and smelt never forgotten, I'm afraid) yet a vet diagnosed it as such. The pup was retained at a vet's for a week undergoing treatment, yet lost its valiant little fight for life. Nevertheless, the vet said, 'It's parvovirus.' I knew different, and told the owner of the dog so. However, something had killed the pup. True, a stomach problem of some sort, and true, the pup had died an emaciated dehydrated skeleton. What then was the cause? Prompted by my curiosity I looked around the owner's garden and found the cause in faster time than it is going to take me to write it – laurel. The dog had apparently chewed enough of it to knock over a Hereford bull, never mind a pup!

Beware of poisonous plants, take preventive action – take them out and read up on toxic plants in a book to be sure. You will find many, probably too many to cope with, nevertheless you will be a lot wiser as a result.

Common diseases and injuries

Perhaps the biggest potential killers of all dogs, Bedlingtons included, are the commonest of all the diseases, distemper, leptospirosis, hard pad and parvovirus. Equally so their eradication is very simple – inoculate against all of these, a simple injection is all that is needed and yet you would be surprised how many ignore this precaution.

Working dogs all through their lives are at risk of sustaining injuries while working. Nowhere is this more so than in the world of the working terrier. Most of the quarry species (with the exception of rabbits) bite back and working terriers with working injuries are a part of life. Ratting terriers are always getting bitten and of course this reinforces my earlier advice about inoculation against leptospiral jaundice, otherwise known as Wiels disease. Despite the fact rat-bites do cause leptospirosis, it is also the rat's urine that is a source of this disease. Do not be complacent, treat all rat bites (even on an inoculated terrier). Dettol and T.C.P. are as good as anything for treating these after they have been cleansed of dirt, etc. The same applies to fox bites; clean them and treat them

95

in this way. Slash or gash-type wounds rarely go wrong, it is puncture wounds that need to be watched and that applies to puncture wounds sustained while working fox or by accidental kennel fights with other terriers. Antibiotics are the answer for puncture wounds, as they get into the blood stream of the terrier and combat infection. Oxytetracycline tablets or an injection of this is usually administered to the animal by the vet.

Although it is impossible for me to elaborate on every conceivable thing that may happen to a Bedlington terrier, either at work or play, I hope this chapter has been a help and a basic guideline. Keeping a dog can be great fun – it can be costly too, at the end of the day. But let me say this – do not begrudge paying your vet's fees when your dog is sick because, in the end, it's your Bedlington's health that is the all-important issue.

Copper toxicosis
When Roy Mee of Leicester mentioned he was going to have his dogs tested for copper toxicosis, I admit I had never heard of the ailment in Bedlingtons. My questioning of various vets revealed very little in the way of information, other than your own vet booked an appointment and you took the dog to Cambridge for the biopsy. No other way other than biopsy was available to diagnose a carrier or affected animal, and the odds were stacked against you having a clear animal. Quite apart from seeing Roy Mee's Roddy all stitched up after the operation and asking Roy how it had all gone, I really never gave it a second thought, although I knew the show people were giving it a great deal of their time both here and I believe in the USA.

When the Working Bedlington Terrier Association was being formed I wrote an open letter to *Shooting News* stating very basically the ideals behind a club or association catering purely for the Bedlington as a working animal. In one part of the letter I made reference to the show-type dog's undesirable characteristics as a working terrier and also mentioned the scourge of copper retention. Knowing copper retention (a condition where the liver retains copper) was proving a headache for the show people, I merely asked why risk breeding them to working dogs? Dogs I might add that had ancestors who lived to good ages and had never shown any signs of dying through a mystery illness. Quite apart from their other undesirable characteristics I could not see any reason why one should use a show dog that might have this ailment.

A few weeks later a series of letters concerning copper retention appeared in this magazine. Without going into the ins and outs of the various opinions given, including my own, it was stated that no Bedlingtons anywhere were proven to be free of the ailment.

The situation regarding Bedlington hybrids becomes a little clearer when one examines the evidence given to me by the University of Cambridge where I believe all biopsies are at present carried out. Assuming that the whippet is, and so indeed was classified by Cambridge University most definitely, an unaffected breed, I asked the question of whether the resulting pups twixt a Bedlington and a whippet would be affected by the ailment. If a Bedlington terrier were either affected or a hetrozygote carrier, at least some of the puppies would be carriers; however, because the whippet is unaffected by the condition, none of the offspring would be clinically affected. That is a better proposition than mating two Bedlingtons, either carriers or affected, together.

It works equally as well if one were to pair a fell terrier or a Glen of Imaal in a bid to improve the Bedlington. The fact that most working enthusiasts of the Bedlington only pair first crosses to either Bedlingtons from lines of dogs that have ancestors that have made old bones, or hybrid dogs, may seem unscientific to some, however I believe it is a more natural and less costly way of eliminating the disease. It would certainly be interesting to see what the results would be of a three-quarter bred animal were it to be biopsied.

The whole procedure that is being followed by the show people in eliminating the disease does show they certainly care about the ailment in their dogs and all credit to them for it; the procedure of biopsy in the first instance and test mating thereafter must be a very traumatic time for them, as success at present is minimal. *The Liver Malfunction Report, 1985*, by Mrs Fiona Craig of the Bedlington Terrier Association, was an ambitious enough piece of writing; I am sure it is depressing for all concerned that the great majority of the show breeders do not have their dogs tested. One clear dog from every breeder was the target aimed for in this report. Subsequent events have proved this to be anything but the case so far. It is very depressing and indeed bears mute testimony to how desperate the situation was when the report was released (and still is) – especially when one knows the very limited number of basic Bedlington strains they have at hand to use. Obviously when at last a clear dog was announced, the show world shouted it from the roof tops, naturally overjoyed at this apparent breakthrough. Steve Lockett's Fantastic Lucky Blue was announced as the first clear dog proven by biopsy and test matings.

Perhaps, at this stage, it is expedient to describe the clinical signs of chronic progressive hepatitis (copper retention) in Bedlingtons. Basically three forms exist, in varying degrees of severity. The first is an acute form, which usually affects young adults. Predictably either sex is at risk and the illness runs a fairly short course, its end being invariably death. The clinical signs to look for are as follows: lethargy, anorexia and severe vomiting. If the dog survives longer than a few days jaundice may appear (apparent on gums, eyes, stomach, etc.). There is no cure – death is inevitable. Stressful events are often blamed for bringing on such symptoms, e.g. whelping.

A second form is diagnosed chronic and this is often the form of disease the middle-aged dog falls prey to. They develop a slowly progressing and debilitating type of illness. The clinical signs are very similar to type one, except that they are present longer (as the dog usually survives longer) and are generally less severe. Weight loss and ascites are often noticed later on in the course of the disease.

Form three is termed clinically asymptomatic form. This particular variation can be detected only by biochemical tests or by the biopsy itself – in other words it is not visually detected. Certainly many would say that if no Bedlington is showing signs then this is the type that possibly affects them, enthusiasts who do not subject their dogs to biopsy may say that if it does not show itself long term, the dog is not at risk. Obviously both arguments have a degree of validity about them.

Blood counts on Bedlingtons reveal that all Bedlingtons, affected and unaffected, are exactly the same, neither do urine tests seem to indicate anything amiss. Biopsy is at present the only scientific proven way (to use the show-folks' words) and of course, for the show people who need Kennel Club registration to exhibit their dogs it is the only way forward as they cannot possibly engage in outcrossing programmes to other terrier breeds.

So where does this leave the aspiring owner of a working Bedlington terrier? To answer this I make no apology in once again quoting the most respected of all the present-day working Bedlington enthusiasts, Mr George Newcombe of North Yorkshire. In a letter, George said to me, 'I have never had my dogs tested, neither has John Piggin, nor did Mrs Williamson; why should we, when they have never shown any signs of having liver trouble?' What I do bear in mind is that neither George Newcombe or Mrs Williamson introduced modern show-breeding stock into their lines, in the case of George Newcombe's dogs, within approximately the last 20 years.

Personally I would not use any modern show dog irrespective of its record from a biopsy and perhaps the last word ought to come once again from George Newcombe, a person in a position to compare modern show breeding with the show dogs of the immediate post-war years, 'It's not the liver disease that puts me off them, but simply that I do not regard the modern show-type dog as a real Bedlington'.

—9—

Breeding

I WONDER HOW MANY of you at one time or another have planned potential litters before your bitch comes into season and have thought longingly about breeding a litter of pups to replace your ever-faithful hunting companion; perhaps a friend or two has said they would like a pup. You may have aspirations of making a few bob or possibly you're just simply curious and would like to try your hand at puppy breeding? Right from the outset let us forget about making a few bob; I know some do, but let me make it clear that most do not and this should be the last consideration. You should breed pups with improvement on the sire and dam uppermost in your mind, or to replace a somewhat ageing working dog.

Colour

From the nest Donna was making it was fairly obvious tonight was the night she was going to have her pups. Donna's belly was well swollen and had dropped back, as all bitches bellies appear to do just prior to whelping. The bitch's time was obviously close, 63 days confirmed this to be the day, as Donna's initial contractions began; there was no doubt that a few hours would see Donna's new family hopefully safely born.

No sooner do those initial contractions begin than the stronger bearing-down pains start, different bitches take varying times to bring forth their litters, Donna is a bitch who had already had a litter so there was no delay and she was soon ready to bring forth the first pup enveloped, as all whelps are, in the foetal sack. Donna licked frenziedly and the first pup gasped it's initial breath.

I knew Donna was out of a liver bitch, and Sam was also sired in turn by a liver dog, but I was a little surprised to see a liver pup, the

100

first to emerge, But not as surprising as it might seem, as two blues mated together that have a liver parent do produce this colour in varying degrees of density, that is to say there is usually at least one in a litter. My surprise was purely down to the fact that I had not really given it much thought and of course Sam being outcrossed there was a possibility it might prove different in this case. Only two other pups followed and these too were liver, which was a little more surprising as there are usually some blue pups (which are black when born) in a litter from blue parents carrying the liver gene.

Perhaps, before we continue the story of these particular pups, the reader would do well to consider some simple genetics to understand a little more clearly some fairly basic rules for puppy planning in litters of Bedlingtons or Bedlington-type pups. If initially we take a liver bitch and pair it to a blue dog that was bred from two blue parents that were themselves bred from blue parents, the original dogs in this example will not carry a liver gene, liver being recessive to dominant blue. Therefore the blue pups in such a litter will be all blue genetically (symbol – BB). This is the dog we are pairing to the liver bitch in this example. See Fig. 1. The symbols I have given are my own personal ones representing each type.

Key
B.L. = Blue cross liver, blue in colour.
L.L. = Liver, genetically all liver.
B.B. = Blue, genetically all blue.

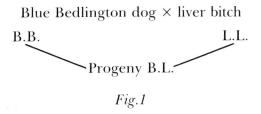

Blue Bedlington dog × liver bitch
B.B.   L.L.
                    Progeny B.L.

Fig.1

Blue dog × blue bitch (but carrying liver gene)
B.L.   B.L.
        Progeny both blues and livers

Fig. 2

101

However, the resulting blues will be all blue as in Fig. 2 (B.B.).

Two livers mated together produce only livers. I have explained how we get a litter of blue in appearance, carrying the liver factor to illustrate how the two blues differ.

Likewise to the liver/liver pairing, if one was to pair only blues to blues (BB) × (BB) you would produce only blues. In genetical type, livers are similar to sandys which is a recognised colour in Bedlingtons. Of course, livers, sandys and blues are not the only colours recognised in the Bedlington terrier; blue and tans also occur, as does the much rarer liver and tan. How then do these bi-coloured dogs occur? One can only hazard an educated guess and say it occurs when several genes come together and certainly for a full answer to this question you would need to seek out a qualified geneticist.

I have seen several examples of blue and tans, Les Robinson's Amy, George Newcombe's Venus, and John Piggin's Ziggy were all sired by George Newcombe's Norman to John Piggin's Lena. Was it Lena or Norman that caused the blue and tan colouring? I don't really know, as both Norman and Lena produced all-blue litters with other partners. I do believe however that Norman did produce a blue and tan with a bitch other than Lena, which does tend to support the theory that Norman carried the gene that causes bi-colours, perhaps both parents need to carry the bi-colour gene?

By the infusion of different genes the likelihood of bi-coloured dogs appears to increase. There is a school of thought that if a person pairs only livers together, washed-out colours eventually result. However, for some curious reason there is quite a vast number of Bedlington enthusiasts who do not like livers, hence quite a lot of blue Bedlingtons exist that are genetically all blue. It is quite rare to get a complete litter of liver pups (as Donna did); when two blues carrying the liver factor come together you expect one or two, but a clean sweep of livers is worthy of note.

When eventually Donna had cleaned her whelps no more even a litter of pups had I seen, exactly the same size and identical triplets. For the next few weeks the puppies did not vary very much in size and truly it was a hard task to choose a pup, however I decided on a really nice red pup which appropriately came to be called Red. George seemed well please with the litter when he came to see them in the winter of that year to take Donna back to Yorkshire.

I never intentionally worked Donna while she was in pup, however she did prove George's point of having quite a nose on her, by catching an odd rat in the lane where I used to exercise her, plus a solitary house mouse which had found it's way into a shed where my pair of lizard canaries were kept. Either way, she proved she could move quite a fair old bit and certainly was nobody's fool. Not only this but she was mad keen to be let loose from a spade she was tethered to once while on a fox dig. I had taken Donna along for the exercise and to get her away from the very well grown group of pups, who by now were plaguing her a little; had I let her off her leash, I am sure she would have tried to get to ground and engage the fox.

Fundamentals of breeding
Breeding a particular breed or type of dog is something most enthusiasts contemplate eventually and the fundamentals of breeding, whatever one's breed, are very much the same. Yet you would be surprised how many people encounter problems that could in most cases be easily avoided.

Readiness for mating
Most bitches come into season at about six months of age and usually every six months thereafter. Certain individuals come in season for the first time at nine, 12 or even 18 months. Twelve-monthly periods are not unusual between seasons, most however do appear to be six-monthly bitches. In irregular individuals a litter of pups can prove beneficial and regulate the bitch to a more set pattern. Counting from when the bitch has shown the first signs of her season (a bloody discharge), at the tenth to twelfth day she will be ready for the dog. Her vagina will swell somewhat and she will indicate her readiness to mate by placing her tail over to one side; if one places one's hands on the bitch's back she will, as it is termed, stand.

The mating
If the bitch is a maiden take her to an experienced stud dog of the working type desired. After mounting her he will eventually penetrate the bitch and tie with her; do not be alarmed with the tie, this is normal. The tie can last from a few minutes to half an hour – 10 to 15 minutes being about average. Hold the tied pair for as long as they are together and do not allow the bitch to drag the dog about as this is not only painful (as the bitch will leave you in no doubt of) but is dangerous to the stud dog. Similarly, if you own a dog and you wish him to stand at public stud, try to let his first bitch be an experienced one – awkward and nasty bitches will do nothing to bolster his confidence, in fact quite the reverse.

The stud fee

What happens after is basically common sense and the run up to most births is fairly straightforward thankfully. After the mating is completed, and most people do not consider this to be so unless the dogs have tied properly, many owners of bitches pay the agreed stud fee on the day of mating, especially in the case of either un-registered stock or other breeds of dog, both terrier or running dogs.

In registered stock, and it must be said a lot of people are petrified of not getting the relevant form signed, a lot of people agree to pay either (a) when the bitch shows signs of being pregnant, or (b) when the pups are born. If you are an owner of a registered stud dog simply do not sign the relevant form unless you have got your stud fee. No money, no signature in other words.

Certainly it is a dubious distinction owning a stud dog for undoubtedly you will meet all sorts of curious folk, thankfully some sane ones as well. If a person turns up with an unregistered dog or another breed, state emphatically before the dogs are brought together that it is cash on the day of mating and have the money in your hand before any contact between the dogs is permitted or else, rest assured, you will learn the hard way. Either you will get a load of empty promises in the form of 'I'll pay you when the bitch shows signs of being in pup' or 'I want you to have a pup instead of a stud fee because I'm broke', or something along those lines which, basically translated, means 'Ta, sucker, I hope I never see you again.' This is why I consider it to be something of a dubious distinction being the owner of a stud dog. Stud dogs are all very well to have at hand when you require one; in most cases, though, it is more economical to hire the services of someone else's.

Exercise and feeding

A pregnant bitch after going out of season should get quite a lot of exercise and not be overfeed; keep her food about the same as normal and whatever you do, do not be tempted to lay her up or overfeed. A classic example of someone who did this springs to mind. The bitch in question was an English bull terrier whose owner stopped walking her and overfed her drastically; eventually when her pups were due, she needed a ceasarian section performed on her by a vet.

From about the fifth week you should be able to see signs of the bitch being in pup, walk her still, especially on roads and on the leash, dose her every day with a teaspoonful of codliver oil (halibut oil or capsules will do equally well). Keep her fit and hard, after all you want to be properly rewarded for all your work by letter and telephone to find a suitable stud dog, also all the time spent studying in depth all the relevant pedigrees and blood lines (you should try to be as familiar with these as you are with the back of your own hand). Success in breeding dogs or any livestock for that matter comes as the result of much hard work and certainly not over night, in other words attempt to become a good stock man.

At about the fifth week of pregnancy, some dog books advocate an increase in the amount of food; for a pregnant bitch of course, it is essential that she should have the correct food to produce healthy whelps and the subsequent milk she will need. On the subject of increasing the bitch's feed it is here I feel that many people make a mistake and get tempted to overfeed. Once again let common sense prevail; do not underfeed, however do not under any circumstances go overboard and feed excessively. Fish oil, either halibut or cod liver oil, as well as calcium in the form of calcium gluconate should be given daily as this will ensure that the right amounts of minerals and the vitamins A and D are present in the blood.

All through the normal 63 days gestation period one must remember to keep the bitch fit and hard. However, a word of caution – after about five weeks do not allow her to jump up on kennels or suchlike (or at least try to avoid this happening). Obviously, as the bitch gets bigger and nearer the end of the gestation period, make sure she does not get the chance. Do not let her indulge in rough play either with dogs, livestock or humans for that matter.

Preparing for whelping

Pups should be born indoors (that includes a suitable shed) somewhere that is draught free and that the bitch is accustomed to. An outside shed is perfectly all right in summer as long as it has got an electricity point, both for lighting and a heat lamp. A whelping box should also be available for the Bedlington bitch which should be large enough for the terrier to turn round easily enough in and to lie out full length. A rail should be attached to the sides of the whelping box just below the level of the Bedlington's back when in a lying position.

Bedding is quite an easy subject to cover; do not use anything coarse such as hay or straw, but use newspaper or some types of cardboard, both of which can, and should be, burned after being fouled either by fluid or blood. After about 63 days, the bitch will become restless, will move about from place to place and will scratch at the floor of her box, shredding the bedding up as she

A Bedlington stands alert showing state of coat when working.

does so – this is all perfectly natural. She may display signs of pain and will probably whine and whimper, all perfectly normal reactions and nothing to be alarmed about. The bitch will, at this preliminary stage of birth, start stretching out at full length, she may well be distressed and will be panting; the labour has now begun.

Whelping
Puppies can be expected within an hour, probably the first within a half-hour. Labour can and does vary in time for individual bitches and a bitch with her first litter will normally take longer than a matron bitch. Of course, at this stage things can go amiss for several reasons. The biggest danger is a bitch not having sufficient contractions to deliver her pups, this is called uterine inertia; I do not think it is more likely in a first-time bitch as some people believe, but suspect it is more likely to occur in a poorly conditioned bitch (i.e. one that has been left to go too soft, or is too fat, or both). Certainly if labour does continue too long (and three hours is long in a Bedlington) without any pups being delivered, for goodness sake call out your vet.

I am happy to say not many Bedlingtons seem to suffer problems giving birth, though of course it can happen, if in any doubt call your vet, he or she will know what to do. Let us hope your bitch is sufficiently fit and so far everything has gone well, the whelp will be moving down to the orifice of the vagina and is now about to be born. It is at this point the foetal sack in which the pup is enveloped usually ruptures. In most cases the pups will come head first, breaches are however by no means uncommon, usually a bitch copes well enough with this, but do watch out to see that no limbs are obstructing delivery, as a little gentle help may be needed in this case, I emphasise, may. The foetal sack will then be licked away and subsequently eaten and the bitch will then bite the umbilical cord.

At this point, I will digress slightly. A person I know recently had a litter of pups from a bitch who absolutely loathed her owner and never let him near the new-born pups (a bull terrier incidentally). When the bitch eventually went outside to empty herself, he examined the precious whelps, and later told me, 'The bitch is hopeless, she's left part of the cord on.' He actually believed that the bitch should bite the cord off at the stomach. I asked him how many litters he had had prior to this, he said, 'Three,' and I then asked him how many pups he had reared from those litters, he said, 'None,' small wonder (sadly this litter also all died).

Back to the labour of our Bedlington bitch. The afterbirth,

which is basically what remains of any membranes and the placenta will subsequently be passed by the bitch. A strong word of warning on the subject of afterbirths – for goodness sake try to make sure the bitch expels them all, failure to do this may well result in complications. For this reason it is always desirable to watch the entire birth; problems occur often as not when a bitch gives birth at night (as most seem to do) and you are blissfully unaware of it all happening downstairs. If you are in any doubt about whether your bitch still retains anything she should not after the births, then call in your vet. Fatal circumstances can occur if there is anything amiss, so for goodness sake be aware of this.

Not too long ago I knew a Bedlington bitch who had delivered two pups in the night and upon examination the next morning nothing seemed wrong, two healthy pups, cleaned up and sucking well. After checking the bitch's vagina it was noticed that she was not passing any blood as is usual; obviously something was blocking up the discharge's exit and closer examination revealed a small fleshy object protruding from the bitch's vagina. A gentle pull (and judging from the bitch's apparent lack of pain this did not hurt her), and an almost complete afterbirth was expelled; had this not been noticed it is almost certain that fatal circumstances would have occurred. Free from the obstruction, the bitch bled, as is normal in a bitch just after whelping.

After producing the first whelp, the rest of the litter should arrive at varying intervals. Some bitches are regular deliverers, other bitches are not so prompt. Bedlington bitches usually seem to be able to deliver their whelps with no serious problems and in most cases nothing will happen to give concern, common sense and an unobtrusive presence seem to be the most sensible way to approach the imminent birth of a litter of pups. Most bitches like to get on with the the birth unaided, but it is advisable to be on hand if possible and in my case I really do think most bitches like to have the company of someone they trust and care for, especially a first-time bitch, matrons know what it is all about.

Let your bitch clean up and lick her pups, let her love them and suckle them, leave her be and let her be quiet, for now her task has really begun in full, namely the rearing of her young Bedlingtons. A lot of bitches like to stay with their pups for quite a time after the birth, it is indeed a good sign, one that shows a caring dam who is unlikely to reject her pups. The pups will be suckling valuable colestrum giving them immunity, albeit temporarily, to diseases. Eventually the bitch will get up from her litter and pass the green-black motion so associated with a bitch who has just whelped, this should not continue after this. The bitch will continue to pass the discharge of bloody fluid for some days yet, decreasing slowly in volume. If it is increasing dramatically, again it is a job for the vet, as this can be the sign of an infection.

Feeding the nursing bitch

For the next few days feed the bitch regular amounts of light food so as not to upset her stomach, cereals or eggs in warm milk, gradually increasing to a more flesh-based diet. I am a great believer in meat diets for all carnivores, one of which of course the dog is, and am always amazed at some ferret enthusiasts who positively scorn the flesh diets I give to ferrets, consisting mainly of rats, mice and rabbits, in preference to the bread and milk diets so often advocated by themselves. Nursing bitches flourish on flesh and now is the time to pump as much in to them as possible in order to rear a strong healthy litter.

Before I go on any further – if you do take the bitch for a walk in the early stages after parturition do not keep her away from the pups for very long as they will soon chill, not exactly beneficial or desirable, I am sure you will agree.

Weaning the litter

After about three weeks those little tiny milk teeth, so needle sharp are beginning to appear and it is time to think about weaning your litter of Bedlingtons. Most pups will lap fairly easily, spluttering, bubble-blowing nostrils, the lot; however it is not long before pups get the hang of it. Milk and eggs being as good a start as any for this version of the liquid lunch. Meat diet can also be started not too long after this. By the way, it is interesting to observe just how early pups will home-in to flesh, even tender mites barely two weeks old, will suck at a rabbit's kidney if you hold one to its nose. Well-cut-up, tender, scraped, lean meat is ideal. Do not over-feed (again that statement) but start at first with one meat meal a day, gradually increasing to two or three depending on how you judge the pups to be coping and progressing. Most pups are greedy, so if possible do not let them overfeed so they become bloated and appear in discomfort. A gradual increase in food is the order of these early days.

By the time they are five to six weeks of age the litter of pups will be on four meals daily and you will have wormed them on a special puppy wormer (following the wording on the packet to the very minutest detail) just after weaning. With any luck you will have picked your pup if you are going to keep one back for yourself. This is always a good sign for anyone who comes to view your pups as potential owners, as it does instil a great deal of confidence in the potential of the litter to the would-be buyer. From six to eight weeks old the puppies are ready to be found homes, and here begins perhaps the most difficult part of the whole process of breeding pups.

Selling the pups
Just as when buying a pup yourself you will now find yourself scanning once again through such publications as *Shooting News* and *Exchange and Mart*. Your advertisement should always tell the truth; if your pups are outcrossed, say for example you have bred a lakeland bitch to a Bedlington dog, state so in your advert, otherwise rest assured, if have labelled them Bedlington pups or Bedlington type you will be rather unpopular with a would-be purchaser when he or she turns up expecting to see a Bedlington bitch with the pups, or even if it is the other way round (lakeland sire, Bedlington dam).

You must be honest with the people viewing the pups, so state the cross in your advertisement. You will soon learn that not everyone wants an outcrossed dog. It is always amazing how many lurcher enthusiasts, so much in favour of cross-bred running dogs, are against cross-bred Bedlingtons. Equally so, if your bitch is a straight-bred Bedlington terrier, instead of a first cross or Bedlington type. Tell the truth, and if people do not like what they see, well that's their lookout.

Never push a pup on anyone, as it is a fair bet, it will not even last six months with them. On the other hand beware of the haggler (the person who tries to bid you down a fiver or a tenner), never give in to them; if your pups are healthy and well reared, it is an insult to you and your bitch – tell them 'no' every time. Then comes the real peach, the person who turns up, tries to haggle, then takes a pup after stating you have already overstretched his price by a tenner or so (conveniently forgetting he agreed to the price told to him over the 'phone) and goes away begrudgingly with the pup.

This reminds me of a story related to me not too long ago by a friend who lives in Wales. Mike had allowed his Bedlington bitch to have a litter of pups, a nice little blue/black bitch, mainly working bred though she did have some show breeding. None the less the bitch had worked rabbits, although she was of a too gentle nature for fox work. She had been paired to a small blue dog and three pups had been the result of the mating. Everything had gone well and the time had now rolled round for Mike to find homes for the pups.

After placing an advert, the two dog pups in the litter had gone within the first day of them being advertised. As it happened they were Kennel Club registered and of course, as such, pure-bred. A couple of days went by and a telephone call from an interested party, all the way from Durham, with the request could they come down to Wales and view the pup. Mike vexed them a little by asking, 'Do you want a Bedlington for working with?' (He had stated 'working rabbiting parents'.) The voice at the other end sounded a little evasive – 'Well, a bit, I know all about working terriers, I used to have a Yorkshire terrier you see.'

Not quite yet put off Mike continued, 'You know what a Bedlington looks like don't you?' 'Well I do yes, I've just looked them up in my book, anyway mate, I ask the questions, can I come down and see the pups tomorrow?' Mike, flustered possibly by this outburst, agreed that the next day, Sunday would be all right to come and view the last remaining pup, a little blue bitch.

Sunday morning dawned bright and clear and Mike was up early enough, keen and eager to make an impression on this somewhat unusual working terrierman who favoured Yorkies. None the less Mike made sure the place was neat and tidy for when at last the party from Durham duly arrived in Wales. Handshakes and the normal formalities were exchanged, Mike proceeded to show them the pup, an average potential-wise, though if it was like it's dam it would make an excellent rabbiting bitch as she was rarely if ever wrong when marking a rabbit to ground.

The person from Durham did not appear like someone who would really want to work the dog at all. After a lot of deliberation and head scratching, the man in question offered to buy the mother of the pups but Mike laughed and refused, politely saying 'No, there's the pup, it is up to you if you want it or not, but if you don't have her I will probably keep her myself'. He offered ten pounds less than the price Mike was asking, did not succeed, and bought the bitch at Mike's price which he was well aware of before he even came to Wales, though on leaving he did tell Mike he had already overstretched him on the price and the speechless Mike was left mouth agape on his front doorstep. The absolute cheek of it all!

Twelve months went by and Mike forgot all about the curious character who had bought the bitch from the litter, although he did see both the two dog pups and they had turned out nice little bushing, ferreting companions, which was what their owners wanted them for and they seemed well pleased with their purchases. However, one morning the telephone rang. 'Hello,' said the voice at the other end of the line, 'can you remember me? I'm the person who bought the bitch Bedlington off you' (how could Mike forget). 'Well,' the voice continued, 'I'm not very pleased at all with her, she has not got a curly coat and she's gone undershot!' Mike asked if there was anything wrong with the dog. 'Look, old pal, I've just bloody well told you,' the voice retorted back.

The long and the short of this tale is, the man who bought the pup, bought it giving the impression that he wanted it basically as a pet, at most to work it occasionally; he explained (or rather ranted and raved) that the bitch was not bred the way Mike had told him and that with a coat like it had got it could not possible be pure bred. The outrageous man demanded his money back on the pup, telling Mike, 'If it is so good, have it back, you told me you were going to keep it anyway.' The outcome of this story is Mike travelled all the way to Durham, bought the bitch back at the price he had sold it for to save any further aggravation (most would not have done so), only for the bitch to die four days later from parvovirus.

Mike, now totally drained, emotionally and physically, never made any attempt to contact the person in Durham about it (he would probably have told Mike it was his fault for not asking for an inoculation certificate anyway) and vowed this was going to be his one and only venture into breeding pups.

Let the reader be reassured that most people, thankfully, are not like this when it comes to giving a dog a good home, and appearances can indeed be deceptive. To coin a phrase, 'You should never judge a book by it's cover', however some odd and peculiar characters come along and the potential breeder of even a very occasional litter should be aware of these people, just as much as the commercial breeder is. Most odd requests are minor ones, for example, regarding a Bedlington litter, 'Are the dew claws taken off?' 'No,' came the reply. 'Well I don't want one, ta ra,' came the sharp retort.

Truly, breeding pups, even occasionally, can be an eye-opening experience. Not that the buyers are always wrong by any means, just as when you are buying anything yourself, be it a car, pair of shoes or a dog, you should only purchase what you think is correct and, it has got to be said, I have seen some miserable and poorly reared pups in the past. When someone does buy a pup off you, tell them about the lines they should be looking for in a Bedlington

A Bedlington bitch waiting while her owner enters a ferret.

that they hope to work, and sit down and explain to them why this is so.

From time to time you will get seemingly reasonable requests like, 'Can I see the mother work?' Equally, there are reasons why you should refuse such a request and any reasonable person will understand them. Most people who want to see a bitch working, or the dog, if you have him, will want to see it go to ground on a fox; but you might not just at that time have on hand a fox to ground and even if you have, sending a dog to ground, as any working terrier enthusiast will know is not exactly guaranteed to take half an hour, which is not particularly convenient if you have someone else calling to see the puppies imminently. Other reasons might be that you do not have ground close by, or you do not have permission to take others on such land, likewise you might not have permission anywhere.

For all these reasons it is inadvisable to say 'Parents can be seen working,' because to state this in you advert and then refuse may well raise doubts in potential buyers' minds. Do however tell the truth and do not make fancy boasts; if your bitch is a good one, simply state so. If not, state your reasons why you have bred with her and why you have bred this particular way to fix a certain physical appearance (i.e. a good coat, head or jaws).

Calcium deficiency

Quite a number of breeders experience a problem that is quite common in bitches – calcium deficiency. Calcium deficiency, or a calcium collapse as it is sometimes known, can be treated easily, but make no mistake, left too long a bitch will die from it and leave you with the inevitable task of rearing orphaned pups.

An initial sign of calcium deficiency is runny eyes and this can often be overlooked, especially if the bitch does tend to have runny eyes anyway. The second sign is for the bitch to be reluctant to go for a walk or leave her bed at all; again this may be overlooked as just a loving and possessive dam. Other signs are a pained walk when out on a lead, a reluctance to go very far, beginning to limp, and a general lack of strength.

The puppies too will be affected; they will always appear hungry. A litter that are born of even size will very soon begin to fluctuate. You will probably lose a pup or two because the bitch is not producing enough calcium for either her milk, or herself. The pups suffer accordingly. The next step in a calcium collapse is that the bitch collapses and cannot walk at all. She will make a pathetic attempt to crawl to you and by now should have long gone to the vet's.

Should a person have been foolish enough not to have contacted the vet (and this does happen, as the bitch will continue to nurse, suckle and clean her pups), the next stage is a coma. When a dog goes into one of these, as a result of a calcium deficiency, it usually never comes out of it, and dies. Mark well this warning and do not let it get to this stage; the runny eyes, weak walk and hungry pups are all the signs you need to recognise an imminent collapse.

The cure for a calcium collapse is a simple, albeit long, calcium injection to the leg the bitch is limping from. You will see improvement within hours, but do not be fooled though, the bitch will limp for a long time after this, and by a long time I mean a few weeks – patience is the name of the game. So very many people think that as soon as a calcium injection is administered all is well again. Wrong. A bitch subjected again to her pups immediately upon returning from the vets will undo all the vet's good work. The vet will advise hand rearing through the day and only allowing the pups back on the bitch at night to take the excess milk away from the dam.

If a litter of pups is approaching weaning age, your vet will advise you to rush that along for obvious reasons and will advise you about hand rearing methods, milk, etc. He may well ask you if you know anyone with a similarly aged litter and a phlegmatic mother to act as a foster mother. One has to be immensely careful and patient where calcium deficiency is concerned but as long as common sense is exercised, then all can be overcome, with no fatalities occurring.

One Bedlington bitch I knew who had two litters, always lost pups within the first week of giving birth; her pups ranged from good to frail, never did you get an even litter with her. She then had a third litter and finally succumbed to a calcium collapse. A subsequent injection from the vet saved her life, her puppies were reared on a foster mother (a lurcher bitch) and only allowed back on the Bedlington bitch at night. This third litter was quite superb and none of the pups died, neither were they frail. Her previous litters had obviously suffered as a result of her susceptibility to calcium breakdowns.

Fred Newman of Glen of Imaal terrier fame views calcium deficiency as fairly avoidable, and it is true, Fred never has problems in this quarter. He puts this down to the fact that he gives an unlimited supply of calves' milk to both the pregnant and the suckling bitches. He also attributes much of his success to natural flesh diets, which in short means – green tripes and sheep's head.

To conclude this chapter on pups and breeding, do try to make sure your pups go to good homes, keep the names and addresses of all new owners and try to keep in touch with them if possible. Keep all relevant letters sent to you reporting on each pup's progress and file them; you will be surprised what interesting reading they make on a cold snowy winter's evening. Tell new owners exactly how old the pups are, so they can get them inoculated at the correct time.

Remember to give authentic pedigrees, issue all the relevant forms with registered stock and be pleased with yourself and your bitch if you know you have made a good job of rearing your litter. Remember, the quality of every litter is not only important for your reputation, it is also beneficial to the cause of the Bedlington. Puppies can be fun, make no mistake; however they can be hard work too, especially when reared properly.

—10—

Working the Bedlington

I AM ASSUMING that if the reader has got this far, he or she is interested in the Bedlington purely as a working terrier. In assessing the work the Bedlington terrier is suitable for, the following is the true picture.

Traditionally it is a true earth dog, one that goes to ground to fox, either to bolt, kill, or draw it. It is an aquatic dog and not frightened of getting its feet wet in order to pursue the mink, that great American invader. It is a rat-hunting dog, a favourite sport of mine. Also it is suited to hunting above ground and flushing out game and vermin from rough cover. For those that get the chance, stoat and weasel are also fair game, and quite a number become adept at other miscellaneous tasks such as squirrel hunting, no easy feat as it happens; taking rabbits squatting in a lamp beam is another of the more unusual pastimes Bedlingtons have been used for. In the past, the Bedlington has also been used for otter hunting, before it became illegal and also the now equally illegal pastime of badger-digging (this can be confirmed from the early picture of the Salters Hall Wood badger dig).

Let me emphasise, in the strongest possible terms, that otter hunting, badger digging and baiting, and also dog fighting are all illegal. A fine leaflet is available to any working terrier clubs, distributed by the National Working Terrier Federation, explaining clearly and simply the basic rules every terrier man should observe; if you are a member of a club and you have not already got this, put a flea in your secretary's ear, he/she will know, or should do, where to get it from.

How does one go about getting a Bedlington terrier pup to start hunting? There are no hard and fast rules, except possibly that he must get plenty of opportunity to develop to his full potential, and

117

.rtunity I certainly do not mean once a month. It
ervation, unlike George Newcombe's, that some
s take quite a bit of time to get going, and I think I
n finding this.

many Bedlington pups or young adults have been
posed of, sometimes uncaringly, simply because their
er had enough patience. This change of owner has then
tally deteriorating effect upon the young adult dog, at a
time . en it should be developing it's instincts in the pursuit of
vermin and game. Ironically such dogs never develop to be good
working dogs because of changing hands rather than a lack of
natural ability and it is a sad fact of life nowadays that some very
peculiar people are simply passing through lurchers and terriers
missing many potentially good dogs on the way.

One chap I knew bought two Bedlington pups and by the time
they had been inoculated and reached 16 weeks of age he had
disposed of one; however, this bitch was young enough to cope
with the move and fortunate in finding an excellent home and
developed from a nervous puppy to a brilliant worker both above
and below ground. It is a fact that there are many people in the
modern terrier and lurcher scene like this dog's former owner, as a
glance around the many summer working-dog shows will prove.
Another point worthy of note is how few veteran dogs, both
terriers and lurchers, are entered for their respective classes at
shows, simply I fear because many dogs over four years of age are
either sold as working dogs or in some cases put down and not very
often by a vet's needle either.

A dog who has served his master well, be it a working, show or pet
animal deserves better and I must say it is here that the show people
on the whole are leagues ahead of the working people; not
everyone is callous but, alas too many are. Of course, from time to
time adult dogs have a bona fide reason for coming on to the
market; I regard such reasons as ill health on the owner's part, or
when someone is limited in the amount of days he/she can work the
dog and to keep a valued line going they lay off a dog to someone
on breeding terms (for future use). Alternatively, particularly
aggressive dogs who can only be worked or kennelled solo (in the
case of the person who owns several animals) often fall into this
category.

Before returning to the Bedlington as a working terrier, bear
with me just a little longer and let me relate what I consider a
very sad tale in which the owner made the ultimate sacrifice rather
than see his failed terrier go from pillar to post. The dog in

question was a Manchester terrier, the smooth-coated black and tan so famous for its exploits (back in the time before they were abolished) in the rat pits of old. The young adult was well developed sexually at the age of 10 months, too much so in fact, as he thought his only mission in life was to breed as many half-bred Manchesters as possible with as many different bitches as possible, even if they were not apparently in season. He was as equally determined to kill (or attempt to) as many male rivals as possible to ensure this mission was accomplished.

The dog had come by his new home with the gentleman in question after disrupting the family life of an elderly couple, living their lives for them and dominating them successfully. It slept on their bed, ate the same food as they did, grew fat and totally pleased itself as to what it did. When eventually enough was enough, my friend acquired it, papers, pedigree (which showed how inbred it was), inoculation card, the whole lot, including an endless supply of choccy-drops (not dog ones either, I think his children ate them). The dog was called, inaccurately, Spot, and was hopefully going to be worked. To cut short a rather long tale of ripped carpets, curtains, etc. (the dog would not sleep outside – when this was tried constant barking proved too much) the following is a brief description of it's tale of woe.

It would go through any cover following my friends bitch Russell, as it was intent apparently on breeding a litter of first cross Manchester/Russells, but never once did it show any inclination to work on it's own. They do say, however, that every dog has it's day, so when at last it was taken to a poultry farm one summer evening and entered into a poultry-free, blocked-exit, deep-litter pen, the dog galvanised into action, killing the bolting rats as they ran to freedom, in the manner of a bygone ancestor from days of old. As a ratter the dog was quite superb – shaking one rat and nimbly on to the next with the dexterity of a seasoned rat-killer – on that night in June I saw him kill 30 plus rats solo.

However, pleased as my friend was with Spot's rat-killing feats, his wife understandably did not find him quite so endearing, as his carpet-ripping, curtain-destroying antics amused the demented unfortunate Spot as much as escaping rats did. Alas, Dave made his decision and had him put to sleep; his explanation was, 'I'm not having him bumped from pillar to post, John, as much as he was a bleeder; I would not have him go to a home only for him to cause trouble and go to another and another'. The ultimate sacrifce indeed, and a sad tale.

It is not the same with many terrier and lurcher owners

119

Trying to get a rabbit out of a tree stump.

unfortunately and I can well recall the lost, bewildered look in one Bedlington's eyes I saw sold at a show by a so-called dealer. It is high time show organisers did something about the so-called dealers turning up at country fairs, etc. with their wares (dogs) on show, and there is one way to stop them – do not buy from them. If that's offended some – tough!

When most people are asked to define a working terrier (or in fact a terrier at all) the majority will say 'A dog that works underground to foxes' and it is true that this is most certainly top of the list as far as the quarry species are concerned, and some terrier men will not work anything else at all. On the subject of legitimate prey, let me define that legal quarry is fox, rat, rabbit, mink and some other smaller prey which need not particularly concern us in this chapter; it most certainly is not (and I want to hammer this point home in the strongest possible terms) otter or badger. Leave both of these, the largest of the British mustelids, alone; disturbing their homes is an offence and that in itself should speak volumes to everyone.

The Badger's Act of 1973 gives full protection for the badger, and the amendment of 1985 means that if the police can convince the magistrates that there is circumstantial evidence that an individual was after a badger it is up to the terrierman to prove his innocence. Perhaps this will illustrate to the beginner that tampering with a sett, digging, or attempting to dig, a badger is not only strictly illegal but could prove costly and under no circumstances should he ever believe otherwise. My advice to any beginner would be at first to go out with an experienced terrierman, as it would be he more than anyone else who would show him the skills of digging fox and their habitats.

Ferreting
Sermon over, now back to the Bedlington. Hopefully you are a caring person prepared to wait, patiently, have got your pup inoculated, coming, sitting, staying on command, knowing his name and of course broken to the ferret, drinking from the same dish and regarding it as a friend by now. Let's assume winter is here and with purse nets, spade, ferret and Bedlington, a frosty morning beckons, up at the break of day and you cannot wait to go. You can smell that rabbit stew already – flask filled, bacon sandwiches packed? Good, let's go. Crossing the old hay meadow where, in the summer, blue butterflies flitted with rather drab meadow browns and grasshoppers chirped, on past the row of oak trees where the cuckoo threatened every warbler and dunnock

brood around and now the newly arrived fieldfares and redwings pillage the hedge of it's hawthorn berries that lead up to the great oaks.

We are nearly there, yes, here is the first warren; it's been a cold night, and all the rabbit pellets surrounding the holes have apparently been deep-frozen. All the time the little Bedlington pup has been taking notice, sniffing the magical smells along hedgerows and ditch bank, not naturally in the manner of a seasoned dog but enough for you to be pleased none the less. You will have or should have noticed this and praised him when he arrived back at your heels.

Having netted up the holes either side of the hedge, you tie the dog to what remains of an old fence, he's sniffed the holes gingerly and again you have praised him, though now you want quiet, so as hopefully you can get a bolt or two. Tell him to lie down while you get out your little jill ferret. With this the dog stands, as he probably thinks it's play time again now his old pal has been brought on the scene; once more you tell him to lie down and he obeys, you have trained him well. Now pop that jill down the hole; with a little shake and a momentary sniff at the entrance she enters the inky blackness of the subterranean world below, ambling off and following her instincts too – like the pup this is her first outing.

You sit back on one knee, away from the view of any escaping rabbits bolting from the holes, and wait. For what seems like an eternity, all is quiet below ground, the pup is impatient like all 6-month old terriers and begins to whine. 'Quiet,' you hiss at him and again, 'Quiet.' This time he stops. You are pulled from your trance like being into the real world, a squeal from the other side of the hedge alerts you as a rabbit has been tangled in the purse net you set on that little bolt hole you so nearly missed. The terrier has heard it too, he barks at it and jumps back frightened as you pass near him to vault over the fence to get to your prize, who by now lies quietly within the confines of the purse net.

The young jill has followed it out and has locked on it; you dispatch the rabbit quickly and humanely by breaking its neck and reset your net, the jill staying at the twitching rabbit's corpe, excited at her first kill; you have been lucky, the first time to ground and success for the little ferret.

Do not force her back and handle her carefully, praise your pup who did not go crazy barking and yapping after that once when the rabbit squealed. He sees you get back over the fence, bunny in hand, put it down away from him, let the ferret worry it again – we are not too bothered if there are any more coneys at home in this warren as this is a learning time for both pup and ferret. Get the ferret away now, the pup seems keen so let him sniff and mouth the rabbit; encourage him, we are not going to be too bothered about this rabbit being damaged a little. As my old uncle, an old-time ferret and dog man used to say, 'Don't mind the bruising, it all adds to the gravy.'

You try the jill again to ground and once again she's down a decent amount of time, but your netting has not been so good this time and a second rabbit hits the net near to you, you bend forward and the rabbit seems to be held only by a leg. With a kick it is free and you miss your prey, diving at it and predictably missing in your excitement; looking up from your horizontal position you see the confused bunny turn past your tethered pup, who, pulling at this new apparition, yaps. You get to your pup and let him loose, 'Go on lad' and in a trice he is off and on his way after the coney. Your jill comes out and you pick her up and secure her in the carrying box, pick up those nets in a minute.

Now to get to your pup, who has followed by sight the rabbit across the meadow and into some blackberry briars, where upon he sniffs and enters the well-worn rabbit run, all through the rough cover he goes and he really is bumping the bushes. A resounding success I would say – in an hour or so you have blooded your ferret and started your pup on rabbits. Of course, not all first outings turn out like this, on some initial hunts you do not even get a rabbit out of a warren, but this time lady luck has smiled. Take your prize home and let the ferret and the dog have some rabbit as well as yourself, and, by the way, do not forget those blessed nets you have left on that bury.

Continued outings and more success at ferreting is beneficial. As the Bedlington gets more and more experienced recognising strong rabbit scent, naturally the better he will get. A knack he hopefully will acquire is marking rabbits below ground, simply by sniffing the warren entrances; different dogs indicate in different ways, some scratch and whine, others just cock their heads to one side and hold a foot up, they vary as individuals. Working rough cover is of course a real cracking way for a terrier to gain experience, developing its scenting ability, for it should always be remembered that a terrier is only as good as its nose. I am quite aware some terrier men upon reading this will hold up their hands in horror, at the mere mention of letting a terrier that is going to be hunting foxes at a later date be used now at rabbit, a point which will be discussed later on in this chapter, in the section on fox hunting.

Bushing

By now your pup will hopefully be hunting rabbits in rough cover but he will miss most if not all of them. As a hypothetical example, if say he was six months old when you first took him ferreting in December, five months have elapsed and it is May, he is 11 months old and since probably early March you have finished ferreting, as the rabbit breeding season has started by then. On the assumption that a young terrier hunting rabbits in cover is as yet hardly the supreme predator, you have continued taking him out – it is good experience for the young dog and all you are doing basically is exercising the rabbits.

I know many people will be vehemently against my next sentence but it does have a valid point if you think about it. One day your terrier, if lucky enough, will catch a young rabbit that is not as experienced as an adult and is just as likely to get taken by any other natural predator. This will be a triumph for your pup, a first real catch for him in rough cover, his confidence will be bolstered. If you are really lucky, an occasional fox can be taken this way, that is if you have a gun or strong lurcher in tow with you on your walks around.

For all the criticism the Bedlington gets in some quarters (and I admit I am only too aware of the problems the breed has), one quality the breed is unsurpassed for is scenting ability. Bedlingtons have quite the most superb noses I have seen on any dog. Andrew Penrose, a rabbit hunter from the Manchester region has a wonderful little blue Bedlington he uses mainly for rabbiting; both Andrew and his brother Robert say that if the bitch marks up a warren it is time to net up and that rabbit stew is virtually guaranteed on the menu. Basically the Bedlington is a great rabbiting dog, no cover is too thick for it and its enthusiasm at rabbiting makes the breed a great favourite among coney hunters.

Many people, including Mrs Williamson, state that the dogs are exceptionally quiet while in the pursuit of rabbits. It was often said that this silence made them great favourites with old-time poachers. Personally I have found most Bedlingtons to be quite the reverse when hunting-up rabbits; they scream like banshees and really do let you know that they are on to something, not such a bad quality when bushing rabbits in conjunction with lurchers or whippets as it is a signal for an imminent bolt and alerts the running dogs. Rabbits that are reluctant to go to ground can often be taken with a great deal of fun and sport by using a Bedlington and lurcher together and I am not ashamed of saying that, for sheer sport and lightening fast dog-work, this type of light-hearted hunting really does take some beating.

Bushing among the rubbish

One particular place I used to have permission to hunt on was a mass of old prams, bicycles, sheets of scrap metal and blocks of concrete. It appeared that the landowner had dumped just about every conceivable type of rubbish that lay about his farm here. Briars grew thickly and as you can probably guess, such a habitat attracted rabbits in their thousands. On arrival at this location at first light, hordes of rabbits would dive for cover – which would be only feet away – among the briars and rubble. To get a good clear course here was practically impossible, so a lurcher that relied purely on sight work was of little use, a lurcher had to use his nose and possess lightening-fast reflexes, as fast as a bushing terrier's to hope for a catch. Yet despite this, my old lurcher Blue took an amazing number of rabbits here, hunting with my friend Dave's Bedlington. Once the terrier picked up the rabbit's line she would bay like thunder, nine times out of ten a rabbit would bolt from some cover – straight into the next piece of cover perhaps only a few yards away. The Bedlington would follow it straight into the said cover, bay again (thus alerting the lurcher) and bolt it again.

Now a rabbit such as this could give you the run-around for several minutes – sometimes the lurcher would get lucky and make a kill early in the proceedings, other times she would not, or would perhaps get a result after the rabbit had bolted on several occasions (a wearing down process). Often as not the terrier would nail the rabbit within a dense patch of cover completely unseen and wrench the unfortunate kicking coney out from within. The number of catches was never high by any standards, with quite a number of blank days along the way.

However, one day while hunting here, the terrier crashed into cover and a rabbit squealed within; as the bitch pulled the rabbit out, Dave stepped forward to dispatch it – first piece of cover on the day – one rabbit. Meanwhile Blue the lurcher had disappeared around the other side of a bush – yet another squeal pierced the air, rabbit number two – our luck was in, and short-lived. I could see Blue now retrieving the live rabbit to hand, equally I could see vividly the blind swollen eyes, 'Myxy,' I said to myself. A voice called from behind me, 'John, this rabbit's got myxy.' I sighed, 'Yes, so has this one,' I replied.

That awful January morning we caught over 50 hopelessly ill and blind animals. Be under no illusion, myxomatosis is a terrible, terrible way for a rabbit to die.

Evidence suggests that rabbits are developing an immunity to this terrible disease, certainly I have caught rabbits apparently recovering from it, that quite apart from perhaps having one eye closed, show no ill effects. In fact their body weights have been close to normal for the average healthy wild rabbit. To be honest, our rabbits at the farm dump never really did recover, and it was not long after this that the farmer decided to sell off the land for redevelopment I believe. Since those days I have seen myxy cases several times, though fortunately the rabbit numbers seem to recover with amazing speed.

Almost 12 months ago in October, I ferreted a solitary myxy rabbit and all through that autumn and into the winter myxy ravaged the rabbit population. Most walks produced a dead or dying rabbit (the fox population had a field day). On New Year's Eve I caught my last myxy coney (one that appeared to be recovering) and up to about April there were very few rabbit signs, let alone rabbits to be found. Then all of a sudden they were back in numbers; every time one went for a walk in the countryside there were young rabbits everywhere, bolting in all directions. Happily these strains of myxy seem to be getting less and less virulent as time goes by.

A day's bushing

The Bedlington and Jimmy the black lurcher dog out of Bedlington ancestors on both sides, were ready and eager for a spot of bushing – never a serious affair by any standards and more likely to exercise the rabbits than to produce a good bag – the best one would usually get amounted to two or three, if lucky that is. However, the early morning, with its fields, dips and hedgerows shrouded with mists and a sun breaking orange, was more than like-minded beings could stand and one must obey the instincts of thousands of years and venture forth in the search of food. Not the type, I hasten to add that we are stereotyped into accepting from supermarkets, but rather the kind that runs and bobs at breakneck speed and has the audacity to wave it's farewell at you with a white flag.

The streets were quiet and no curtains twitched, as two humans and the same number of canines trudged quietly to the old hay meadows, so beloved by rabbits, as in summer their runs indicated in the long grass – grass that whispered in July breezes immediately prior to its mowing and made the art of snaring easy (a method despised by some and accepted by those who know it as an efficient form of pest control when done properly).

At the side of a hill grew gorse, a prickly perch for that most musical of British finches, the linnet, who in his splendid pink

126

Setting a long net prior to ferreting.

The Bedlington ignores the ferret as it leaves the rabbit hole.

127

breeding plumage sang to the world in fervour, a song rivalling that of his cousin the canary, who was developed by man for a long time to sing his threats to rivals from the confines of a prison. No such bounds held our own version of the British canary, for his was the hill, the gorse and freedom, to fly in the hillside breezes and winds and so was ours freedom to walk at liberty and enjoy God's creation and feel at peace with nature.

But nature is raw in tooth and claw and predators exist; just as the stoats and weasels took their toll of voles, mice and young rabbits, vulpines also preyed on these, and old Brock would shuffle along too, the natural vaccuum cleaner, the original refuse collector and quite the most delightful of our larger carnivores. A little owl's corpse lay in the wet grass, a recent introduction to our list of birds of prey; this poor fellow would take no more voles, and we can only ponder on what sealed its fate.

In the next field a hare stirred, his movements quite hard to follow because of the shifting early morning mists, and a covey of partridges broke cover at our feet virtually. Jimmy had no chance, the whirring wings startling not only the dogs but also us. The Bedlington sniffed at a rabbit hole and from her reaction and all the signs around the hole I was fairly sure a rabbit or rabbits were within. Along the hedgerows she moved, tail wagging and nose to the ground drinking in the smell as she progressed, quickening her pace as it got obviously stronger. The slightest yelp of excitement told Jimmy the lurcher of a prize about to emerge; a brown streak bolted out of the other side of the hedge from which Jimmy was stationed – a good choice from the rabbit's point of view as a clear course was impossible.

The dog crashed through the hedge and tried his damnest; however it was a futile attempt and doomed to failure, for the coney was up, away and down a set of holes and sanctuary long before the dog realised he would not succeed.

Along the end of hedgerow we went but, alas, with no success, so we travelled back, still along the same hedgerow, but this time down the other side of it. Despite the Bedlington's continued efforts nothing was forthcoming, so we crossed the old hay meadow again, where thousands of times high-powered lamps have flashed the path for lurcher dogs to close on coneys held squatting in the beam. The nearing copse is circular and the Bedlington entered the sundry cover of gorse on it's hillocks and briars lower down the slopes with hawthorn and blackthorn around its perimeter. The bitch had disappeared, though we knew from her quickening pace in the cover that she was on to something. Jimmy quivered in anticipation, his grey face darkening towards his neck and eventually the black/blue rough body coat so reminiscent and typical of his Bedlington forebears.

Where the copse had been managed and scythed back, our friend the smallholder who owns the land made a pile of waste wood, bracken, old branches and the like, a warm place for hibernating hedgehog and hiding bush rabbits alike. One of the latter, squatting in its sanctuary was evicted by Rita the Bedlington and it was out, right in front of Jimmy and immediately in its stride; off balance, the dog corrected himself and gave chase down an avenue between the hedgerow fence and copse. The course continued, the rabbit flustered by the blue apparition directly behind him did not do the sensible thing and bob; on out of sight the two went, meanwhile Rita was opening up and appeared from out of the cover a few yards away from us.

For a second there was silence and then a squeal, the lurcher had met his target successfully and he returned with his prize, a wide-eyed rabbit. Perhaps not rabbits in numbers or as picturesque a hunting scene as some, today it was a rabbit, quite easily it could have been one of the copse's red foxes that are frequently pushed out; whichever way it was, the combination of man, lurcher and Bedlington doing the jobs they were created for, to hunt the quarry wherever they may be.

Rat
All your hard work should by now be beginning to pay off; your young adult is going on rabbits, is an asset marking up burys when ferreting and now in high summer you wish to try your Bedlington at rat hunting. There is no close season where rat is concerned, it is a worthy quarry and of course should be ruthlessly exterminated. As a harbourer of disease it is surpassed only by the fly, if that.

Directing the training towards ratting
Having a friend who hunts rats is always an asset where Bedlington pups are concerned (or any terrier for that matter) or you may be lucky and already have a trained terrier. Such an animal will really bring on a green puppy quickly, and the mere fact that it will see an adult killing rats will only help to fuel its enthusiasm. There is only one problem with this however, and that is the question of confidence, for every time a puppy takes a pot at a rat it will invariably be beaten to the punch by the trained adult dog and quite obviously this will do nothing to bolster the puppy's confidence. The secret is to let the pup watch a veteran ratting dog

doing the job, and then next time out, just take the pup; it is a fact that you will miss many rats that you would otherwise have accounted for but make no mistake it is a worthwhile sacrifice to make in introducing the pup to rat-hunting. Always let the pup rag a rat corpse and encourage and praise it for doing so. This action is going to be the start of a long working life, or hopefully so.

No pup should ever be allowed anywhere near a rat, or where rats abound, unless it has been inoculated against leptospiral jaundice.

Rats, like rabbits are prolific breeders; as soon as the doe has had her young and cleaned herself up she's off again to be served by the buck and the whole cycle starts again. Rats really are the great survivors and I know places that are cleared by pest control officers only to be inhabited again a few weeks later by a further colony. Rats are ever on the look out for a suitable place to live and take refuge wherever the environment is correct for their survival, so never underestimate the rat's intelligence.

Locally I am constantly asked by members of the public to deal with their rat problems and in many cases in preference to the local pest control officers, simply because, as often as not in these cases, the householder has a cat, a pet dog, other livestock or children and are none too keen on having Warfarin lying about the place. Poisons are not only deadly but quick to put down and it is obvious the pest control officer who has a long list of calls to make will use poisons not only for their effectiveness, but also for his convenience.

It is when one gets a call out to shift a rat or two that the personal touch really comes in and you can show off that little bit; also you can do your own little bit of public relations for field sports – one successful assignment and you will not any longer be regarded as a possible undesirable, poacher or country bumkin – instead you will be elevated to the role of rat exterminator and you will prove to the public at least locally, that field sports is not all people swigging whisky from shot glasses and 'Tally-Ho where's the bloody fox', which is what some folk think, especially those outside field sports.

Time and time again rats have shown their intelligence especially where traps are concerned. For large adult rats, I like to use catch-alive traps, the traditional whole family type to be exact, you only need to catch a rat or two in one of these before other untrapped rodents have figured out that it is not too healthy to enter one. I have laid trails to the trap and even left pieces of bait within it, going as far as putting the bait behind the hook that operates the whole of the mechanism (the bait behind the hook will go, not so the one on the hook). Cages are preferable for all concerned, as pets and children are not harmed by these should they stray too near them, neither are birds that accidentally get caught, and subsequently released.

It really is amazing how often birds do get caught (alongside hedgehogs) in cages, even when hidden well out of sight on secretive rat runs, blackbirds and robins being the main culprits. Cages at least cause the minimum of distress to them and they are liberated unharmed. A way of counteracting the attentions of birds is to use a tomato bait, as birds do not usually eat them while rats love them. In summer it is possible to multi-catch and I have caught two or three small mousy young ones in one catch.

Young small rats are also taken incredibly easily by using a Nipper-type backbreaker or clap trap; baited again with half a tomato, even in broad daylight you can catch rat after rat in a clap trap, so long as it's on a run. An amazing thing is that on most occasions all the young rats will be identical and of one size (excellent food for your ferret). So easy are young rats to approach that I have stood stock still in a place I know rats to abound and had them right in front of my boots, but move once and of course they will bolt along their runs.

Occasionally one of your ratting assignments will warrant the use of a dog and doubtless here is your chance to try your Bedlington. But, this can be considered only if your terrier is not acting the fool in a puppyish manner and is broken to cats. Most Bedlingtons not brought up with cats as pups are the very devil to break to felines, so a word of caution in that direction will not come amiss. The idea is to try and figure out which way a rat will make good its escape, provided you can get it to bolt. Rats will often be taking refuge under a shed or sometimes paving slabs, bricks, etc. A typical hunt is re-constructed below.

Suburban rat hunt
Mrs Wiltshire has seen a rat while hanging out her washing in her back garden before leaving to go to work, approximate time 6.30 a.m. She has seen the rat on about six mornings now, she also knows Dave to be a competent rat catcher (he caught an old buck rat for her about 12 months ago, in a cage). Could he come and have a look as she does not want the official rat catcher to attend because her cat might catch a poisoned rat. This is a fairly typical request.

Saturday morning duly arrives and Dave and myself turn up with my two ferrets and his two terriers, a Russell type bitch

Marking a rabbit in some scrap iron.

Marking rabbits in a disused barn.

(Penny) and his blue-black first cross Bedlington/fell bitch (Raven). A check round the patio reveals three holes one side of the patio burrowed just under the slabs. The other side of the patio reveals just one hole. To the right of the patio runs a brick wall, six feet high and at its base a well-used rat run. We check to see where the rats will hopefully bolt; at one end of the run is a gate and at its base is a gap by the bottom hinge big enough for an adult average sized rat to get through – this we block with a ball of rolled newspaper. The other end of the patio is another possible escape route, the rats have to run the gauntlet of the open space of a well-mown lawn which they obviously do use under the cover of darkness because at its perimeter the run still shows clearly. About half way along the garden, the next door neighbours' lawn ends and their vegetable patch begins; the rats obviously go among the plants of purple sprouting broccoli planted here.

A polecat jill, a seasoned ratter not yet jibbing, is entered in the hole from the right-hand side of the patio, it is the only one this side. Penny the Russell goes with me while Dave enters the jill and we wait by the gate. Raven patrols alongside Dave and will need to be pretty nimble if a rat decides to bolt as it will undoubtedly go towards the broccoli patch. Not a minute has elapsed, and a young rat still in juvenile coat bolts, followed closely by two more, two away to the left and Raven (and one towards Penny who is being held by the collar by me; half way towards us it turns back into one of the other holes) Raven has intercepted both the others, killing the first with a deft flick and only just getting the other one in its mouth before Penny duly arrives and they are both claiming it as theirs. At that moment another rat explodes from the hole the lucky youngster escaped down, a call from Dave alerts the terriers and Penny takes it; shortly after the ferret appears at the mouth of the hole.

Three bolts and three kills – not bad under such circumstances. Hunting like this rarely produces large bags, and there are some who would scorn such sport. Mrs Wiltshire is delighted; however where there are youngsters there are adults, and that run looks very well used. Dave sets a cage at the end of the patio by the lawn and also a couple of Nipper-type back-breakers next to two holes before we leave. Dave goes back next morning after his Sunday morning stroll to the newsagents; the result – one large doe in the cage and one more young rat, killed cleanly in the Nipper. The traps are left there the rest of that week and checked daily by Dave as he works night shift regularly, but no more rats are taken and by the way the run is drying up, obviously there are no more rats at home. The holes are blocked up. Perfect results, and end of tale.

Now, why would any sane person catch somebody else's rats free of charge and be so apparently keen to do so? Dave estimates he's killed well over 1000 rats in this fashion in about the last 12 months and, as he says, 'It's 1000 rats my dogs would never have killed had I not done it'. Also of course, it is experience for your dog at ratting and the more experienced he gets the better he will be; you will gain experience too, and situations like the one mentioned can occur round farms, in the countryside, absolutely anywhere – so do not knock it. But one chap who used to write from Scotland, said, 'If you hunt rats up here people regard you as being in need of some kind of medical attention.'

Country rat hunt

To attempt to hunt rat really seriously and to take large bags, you will first need to find a suitable ratting site such as a pig or poultry farm or a slaughter house. One place that springs to mind, though sadly it no longer exists in its old form, was at one time an absolute rat-hunters' dream, for rats were present in super abundance. The site was in fact a few acres of ground formerly owned by an old chap who had kept pigs in, let it be said, slightly natural conditions; the sties were rickety old affairs made from old stone walling and bits of concrete, with roofs of corrugated metal and asbestos.

When a friend bought the run-down cottage and the land, surrounded by small woods and copses, he thought it idyllic and set about doing up the old place with a vengeance. Those pig sties were the last thing on his mind as he set about the renovation of the cottage. On the first day working there he saw a cock pheasant and a couple of rabbits sitting in the very over-grown garden, and when next he saw me, he said, 'You would love it over there, John, come over next Sunday and have a look round.'

More through manners than any great interest I went over the following Sunday afternoon. Sure enough the place needed some work on it, though obviously it had great potential. I was watching through the window and my friend's wife had just pointed out the spot where the pheasant usually appeared and added that they had seen a fox on several evenings cross over the road opposite and into their garden. Just then I caught sight of something up by the derelict pig sty – a large ginger cat was playing with something in the long grass. Sophie noticed my disinterest in her chatter and saw me focusing on the tom cat up by the sties, 'It's the fox, it's the fox,' she shrieked. 'Bloody fox,' I laughed, 'it's a cat and it's caught something.' 'I hope it's not Pickles,' she blurted. 'Pickles?' I answered, somewhat puzzled, 'Yes, that's what I call the rabbit I see up there.'

By now I was at the cottage door and making my way up the garden, with Sophie and Adrian, her husband, in tow behind me. Sure enough, upon our approach the tom cat got up and high-tailed it off with it's prey in it's mouth; by now I could see it was not Pickles but a large rat the cat had got. I said 'It's not Pickles that's going to be the ginger cat's dinner, it's a rat.' Hysterics and a hasty retreat by Sophie, running as fast as her little legs would carry her down the path and back to the fortification of the cottage.

Round the pig sties were rat runs and burrows that led quite obviously into and out of the rickety affairs; runs, like miniature rabbit runs in the long grass were everywhere. I peered through the broken window of the sty and, after accustoming my eyes to the gloom, I was greeted by the sight of approximately a dozen average to large-sized rats; they all just sat there apparently completely unconcerned. 'Adrian,' I whispered. I turned my head but he had gone, apparently as petrified as his wife. The rats then bolted, with several queuing up, as is usual, to get down one particular hole, and jostling each other in a bid for safety. For the first time that afternoon I felt greatly indebted to Adrian and Sophie, certainly this rat haven would need seeing to. The rest of the afternoon I spent looking around the other sties and all were similarly infested; I estimate on that afternoon I must have spotted about 200 rats, in daylight, although of course it was quite dark and gloomy within the confines of the sties.

Nightfall saw me back with Dave and the illustrious Raven, his Bedlington/fell bitch and also two Bedlingtons (Raven's sire, Mad Ratter and a small blue bitch called Tina). We both had home-made lamping outfits, used primarily for night-time rabbit hunting, that would do well enough for rat hunting. Remembering as best I could where most of the escape holes were, both outside and inside the sties, I set to work blocking them will balls of newspaper. This done we re-opened the first door, switched on the lamp and the dogs steamed in with Raven, Tina and Ratter all slaying with dexterity and efficiency; 24 killed and many more escaping through holes I had missed in the darkness due to our ignorance of the new hunting ground. The other sties followed the same pattern but, none the less a total of 115 rats between three terriers was not bad, especially when one considers we were missing many holes in the dark.

Consequently bigger hauls were taken on subsequent visits as we got to know the ground better; not only did we storm-troop the rats

135

in the way just described but we also ferreted, trapped and eventually poisoned them, so great were their numbers. The pigs might have been long gone, but their comrades in the sties had lingered on. Eventually, after poisoning the remaining rats the bulldozer moved in and flattened the place Adrian and Sophie called 'rat corner' and Dave and I called 'Heaven on Earth'.

Ratting with terriers, be they Bedlingtons or other breeds is not only great sport and fun, but can also be quite efficient and I have great admiration for a good ratting dog. Scorn if you must, but my conclusion is this: rat hunting not only encourages a terrier to use his nose, but it also sharpens up a dog no end. I have seen many different breeds ratting – Bedlingtons, Russells, Glen of Imaals, Staffords, Manchesters, cairns, borders, a show lakeland and even whippets and lurchers. All showed great enthusiasm at rat and all also displayed great courage, which is something they need in plenty when they encounter their next foe, the great red devil, Charlie fox himself.

Fox

You would probably be surprised how few people actually regard Bedlingtons as fox-hunting terriers, especially in the southern shires and my own native Midlands, and it is here the Bedlington is playing away from home and the Jack Russell type of terrier reigns supreme, in fact so much so that up to the end of the 1970s even the coloured terriers so popularly referred to as patterdales and fell terriers were practically unseen in the south. Most Bedlingtons were show dogs and any dog with a good length of leg was viewed with scepticism. To a certain degree this has not changed very much. I was brought up with Jack Russell terriers, my grandfather's brothers and their father before them all had and worked Russells, and I must be totally honest and say that the best working terrier I ever saw, though only just ahead of the one in second place (a Bedlington incidentally) was a Jack Russell type.

The North of England, particularly Yorkshire, the Lakes and Northumberland are notable strongholds for Bedlingtons and are steeped in the fox-hunting tradition. Wales is often credited as being a great producer of fox-hunting Bedlingtons but despite the fact that Mrs Margaret Williamson and her beloved Gutchcommon Bedlingtons resided near Neath in Glamorgan, I cannot agree with this credit. Bedlingtons are popular in Wales this is true, but there is little evidence to support its being a fox-hunting Bedlington stronghold. In fact I would say Wales is very similar to the English Midlands in its working terrier fashion, with the Jack Russell types

136

Entering a Bedlington into a drain.

remaining ever popular. I know quite a few people in Wales who have got Bedlingtons; most use them for rabbiting and ratting, or as a base line for producing a lurcher, all perfectly legitimate roles for a Bedlington. However, it is a shame a few more do not use them to ground on foxes – they would be surprised.

Without doubt, Bedlingtons will work foxes competently provided one has got the right kind of Bedlington, that is the working type. George Newcombe has a reputation as a person whose kennels have consistently produced good workers over a period of years and many of his Bedlingtons have seen action below ground to fox, after all George himself has worked his own dogs with various North Yorkshire packs, Bedlingtons and lakeland terriers alike. Some of his dogs have been larger specimens than might be imagined, but these dogs are moor dogs, leggy, big and strong and ideal for dealing with foxes in rock. Leggy and big they may be, but also in evidence are clear-cut narrow fronts and laid-back shoulders, an essential quality for a viable moor dog. These narrow fronts and good shoulders work equally as well in the Midlands, the South or Wales. I know a 17-inch high dog with these qualities that works Midland foxes with no real problems; he is narrow and strong, invariably when up to his fox he kills it and often draws it. Many people, however would not consider such a large dog a terrier.

The show people have done nothing to enchance the Bedlington's image as a fox dog, as some quite simply state that Bedlingtons are not earth dogs at all and were never designed to go to ground, while others state that the show dogs are still competent at dealing with the fox underground, though a mere glance from the very greenest newcomer to the working terrier scene will reveal this myth for what it really is.

As previously stated, few people outside Bedlingtons regard the breed as an underground terrier for fox. Despite this, some terrier men do use them, Bert Gripton's Bedlington (and I know absolutely nothing about the animal) is said to be a dog that goes to ground on fox, George Newcombe's Rillington Norman, his old Bedlington/lakeland hybrid was another, as is Tarka his superb liver dog (another first cross), both have seen hunt service. Of course, George's famous old dog Rillington Rinty was an absolute raging fiend at a fox, as has been mentioned previously. Both Rinty and his daughter Darkie (Rillington Rarity) were born fox slayers and had the rounded bottom jaw George so favours.

On the subject of strong bottom jaws being fully rounded, George said, 'I once heard Rinty cracking a foxes jaw up like he would a bone, and Darkie once chewed the whole bottom jaw off one' (let me stress both foxes were completely dead when this occured). Recently George tried the Bedlington cross border as an experimental outcross, and in one letter he remarked to me that a man who obtained one of the subsequent pups from the Castle-ford area was extremely pleased with it and that the terrier in question had self-entered to a fox and stayed with it for three hours.

In some of the non-hunt parts (that is to say no fox-hunt rides over it) of the Midlands and more especially where sheep farming is scarce, foxes are fairly well tolerated and not only exist but thrive. With no hunts, no sheep to speak of and all poultry in fox-proof batteries, Reynard poses no real threat and so is often left alone by the farmer, such conditions being greatly appreciated by the red ones. You would not believe how easy it is to find foxes above ground in such areas in the middle of the day. Terriers hunting rabbits regularly push a fox out and, encouraged to give chase, usually start to regard them as prey. Our old friend the lurcher will usually course a fox, and if he can hold or kill it the terriers should be allowed to rag the kill. On many such occasions foxes are pushed to ground, and the terriers self-enter and you can bet your bottom dollar that it is the time the fox will not bolt when you have not got a spade with you, as you thought you were out bushing rabbits.

Speaking of digging, George Newcombe once said it is a real terrier that can enter an earth on his own and bolt the fox un-aided, which is perfectly true especially in the case of a fox that is to be chased by hounds, as it needs to be uninjured so ensuring a good run and giving the fox a sporting chance to get away and to provide sport another day. Equally, one can net foxes that bolt, or better still I think is bolting them for lurchers; however, often digging is essential in most cases of pest control when the fox must be taken as it is causing a nuisance. Whatever the task, the Bedlington is a viable fox dog and given the opportunity can and will work them. Although many terrier men voice the opinion that a terrier that works fox should be broken to rabbit, plenty still let them work rabbit. Certainly I have faced criticism for hunting rabbits, however I have found that terriers encouraged to hunt rabbits from an early age invariably turn out the best in the long run as fox dogs and any hunting is beneficial as it teaches a dog to use it's nose. If it is a disadvantage it is one I am prepared to put up with, for as the old saying goes, a terrier is only as good as its nose.

Entering to fox

Without a doubt, the best way of entering to fox is by going out with an experienced terrier man and letting your dog see what is required of him. Even if you haven't got such a friend at hand, finding an obliging person need not be such a hard task. In these days with the many terrier and lurcher clubs about, such people can be found by joining one and telling a reliable member (namely a committee man) your plight; you will sooner, more likely than later, get an invite out to see how the job is done. This is ideal grounding for beginner and terrier alike. Not only this, but a reliable, seasoned terrier man will hopefully know what signs to look for and avoid. I am, of course, refering to badger setts and signs and, as already mentioned, an excellent little card is available from The National Working Terrier Federation giving the beginner precise and accurate details of exactly what to avoid. These should be readily available and most club secretaries know where and how to obtain them.

Basically, these cards set out to tell the would-be terrier man what to look for as the sure signs of badger, such as the regularly defined runs or paths to latrine pits, badger tracks (different to fox pads – five claw marks as opposed to the four of the fox), the characteristic bedding at sett entrances, trees scratched and badger hair (black-tipped, coarse and grey) which, advises the card, might be found on barbed wire or on bushes and low trees.

Problems do occur though, mostly because of early entering; a dog should ideally have been allowed to rat for a season or two and have been allowed to prove that he is ready to go to ground to fox and that he is game enough for this new venture.

A word of caution though, do not do what one tyro hunter did not long ago with his Bedlington bitch – he entered her in a fox earth and then promptly entered another seasoned dog behind her. Not only was she pushed up to her fox and suffered badly, she was also repeatedly bitten from the rear by the other terrier (who was attempting to get over her in order to reach the fox). The story goes that the bitch killed her fox and the fool bragged of his bitch's prowess at her first (and only) kill. However, his joy was short lived, for at her next outing she refused to enter the earth; small wonder, and a classic example of an idiot with a terrier.

Using nets

Foxes can be netted just like rabbits, bagged and subsequently released. In these days of anti-field sports movements and all country sports being under fire, perhaps, it is worth pointing out that not all terrier men are the blood-lusting savages some would have us believe. It is only the mindless few that create this impression. Terrier shows, a shop window to the world, attract a whole range of individuals and it is so often at these very events that opinions are forged of the terrier and lurcher fraternity as a whole. To be perfectly honest, some people are hardly helping the cause of field sports, in fact they are probably doing quite the opposite.

The majority of people who hunt foxes abhor their destruction, but problem foxes do exist and on these occasions the death of a fox is unavoidable. The fact is that foxes are on the increase, especially in our urban areas and the stories of city-centre foxes in Birmingham, London, Bristol and Sheffield are too numerous to mention. Often it is here that a terrier man is asked to help deal with the problems which arise because the fox which lives in this environment has had more chicken dinners than his country cousin due to chickens being kept outside, in contrast to the battery houses of the intensive farmer. Problem foxes in urban areas make so-called earths anywhere suitable such as under sheds and outhouses, even below buildings and in vents, etc. As long as the refuge is safe and there is enough shelter, urban foxes will capitalise on such places to live in. Netting such foxes is possible in many instances, although in some locations this can be difficult and it is here that a hard type of lurcher can prove useful.

Using lurchers
Practically any type of lurcher will suffice as long as it has a reasonable amount of guts and the bottle to dispatch its quarry with the minimum of fuss. Over a period of time I have seen all sorts of crosses and pure-bred gazehounds with a natural flair to dispatch foxes. Pure-bred greyhounds, salukis and deerhounds all wed to fox-coursing with the minimum of fuss and I have seen a number of collies that are exceptional foxing dogs. Collie/greyhounds make good enough foxing lurchers as do the sundry terrier/greyhound hybrids. At one time bull terrier/greyhound hybrids were very much in demand as hard type lurchers and much prized by lampers to tackle foxes in a beam. Many of these Staffordshire bull terrier stud dogs were lithe, agile and leggy; the problem was that the show craze was producing a different type of dog, however, enough of the leggy agile type are about which means this variety of lurcher has survived and it has enjoyed a revival in these days of plentiful urban foxes.

With the advent of the American pit bull terrier arriving in

141

A Bedlington bitch chasing a rabbit.

After catching the rabbit.

Britain, even bigger bull/hybrid greyhounds were produced; such no-nonsense dogs are highly prized by the foxing men and are perfect partners for a foxing Bedlington or two. Kerry blue/greyhound hybrids have an excellent track record as fox-coursing dogs and the Kerry's reputation as a game dog is well known and, with an exceptionally thick skin, this type of hybrid may well produce an ideal dog to course foxes with.

In assessing the various crosses, no book like this would be complete without reference to the merits of the Bedlington/greyhound hybrid as a fox-coursing lurcher, and although I discuss in another chapter the Bedlington-bred lurcher, I believe it should be mentioned in this section how such a dog may well be achieved. The greyhound half (in any cross) should be a retired track or coursing bitch, its other half should be a largish working dog (of genuine working breeding). A dog like the late Roy Mee's blue Bedlington dog Dick (around 17½ inches high) or George Newcombe's Blue would be ideal as a Bedlington stud dog in the production of a foxing Bedlington/greyhound hybrid.

A viable fox dog

One day when I was fishing, a barge (yet another one) chugged along the waterway, swilling up the bottom and churning the whole swim into a silty mess. I cursed, 'Be no good now, too many boats,' and sent a scornful look at the boat now passing through. A dog jumped up on top of the barge, 'A blue and tan Bedlington,' I said to myself, with so much of a look of surprise on my face, that the man steering the boat raised his hand, 'How do?' he called to me, 'Alright,' I said, nodding my head. 'What a cracking dog,' I thought. To my astonishment the barge stopped and moored up. 'Any good?' the elderly gentleman called. 'A couple of perch and a gudgeon,' I said, brushing away the question. 'Your dog,' I said stabbing a finger in its direction, 'A Bedlington.' 'Yes,' he said 'an old-fashioned one.' 'Yes, I know,' I replied, walking along the bank for a closer look – 'A gypsy-bred dog, bought it from Appleby.' 'Has he got a pedigree?' I said. 'No, I never got one with him, the man I bought him off couldn't read or write and neither could any of his family who had kept the breed for years. He just kept talking about the Moorhouse dog' (one of the early dogs) 'and how this dog could be traced back to it; couldn't read or write but he could tell you about his breeding, he could – 'been in his family for years' – he kept repeating, 'Always kept 'em they 'ave.' That is probably the nearest one will get to the mythical unknown strain (something

I do doubt exists despite this), never the less it was a crying shame such an animal never had a pedigree to check against.

I packed up the fishing tackle and Eric (the dog's owner) invited me aboard the barge and for several hours we had a good old natter about Bedlingtons. His Bedlington Dogger had been to fox regularly accoridng to Eric, certainly his facial marks supported this statement. As an animal, Dogger certainly looked impressive, a better blue and tan I have definitely not seen; at 15 inches high Dogger was a really viable fox-dog. When Eric left and went on his way I felt more than a tinge of envy for the man who owned that super dog. 'I'll be along here next year again, hope to see you then,' Eric had waved. To be honest I did not hold out much hope of seeing the traveller again.

Twelve months passed by and I was throwing a Devon minnow (an artificial fishing bait) up the waterway with no luck, when there was a swirl at my feet as the pike struck, missing the lure by a fraction. I re-cast and purposely slowed at the same spot and with all the luck in the world the predator struck and the trebles slammed home. *Esox Lucius* the great hunting pike jumped clear of the water shaking her head in a vain attempt to throw the hooks that held her. 'Nice baked in butter they be,' said a voice behind me. I was just about to say 'Get lost,' when I recognised the voice. 'Eric,' I laughed, half turning my head. 'Though not that one,' Eric smirked as the trebles relinquished their hold on the fish and the minnow landed in the tree behind us. Simultaneously we both laughed. 'How are you and where's Dogger?' I asked immediately. 'Lost him, a cave-in, suffocated him and his fox. In Cumbria it were; still miss the old bugger I do.' The sorrow was etched on Eric's face. 'Mind you, I got a pup by him out of a lakeland bitch, blue and tan an' all, gonna be like ol' Dogger I'll be bound.' Eric's face had brightened up somewhat as he told me about his pup.

The making of a hard dog
Having now given examples of some foxing Bedlingtons and the perfect partners for using in conjunction with them (on occasions), perhaps it may be beneficial to give a true account of the entering of one Bedlington terrier to fox, from the time the dog was elevated and promoted from rat hunting to entering to fox. The Bedlington in question was a liver-coloured animal known appropriately as Rusty. He was all working-bred and purchased from a breeder of notability at the age of eight weeks, complete with authentic written details. Like most male puppies he was a silly little bundle of fur for what seemed an eternity. Nevertheless, Rusty had proved to be a

144

willing student, accepting and learning his basic commands with the same amount of training as any breed of terrier. From the time the pup had a full set of adult teeth, he was taken out with his owner's border terriers, ratting alongside them and, with a little patience, the young Rusty learned his trade.

With a much-bitten muzzle and greatly improved nose, the autumn arrived. Rusty, now approaching his first birthday was given the opportunity to go rough-cover hunting with the border terriers and a collie cross greyhound lurcher. The dog had shown reluctance to enter the sundry cover, pulling back from every briar that tugged and snagged at his profuse, light-coloured top-knot. This was duly clipped away and now with no such impediment to hold him back he followed the borders into cover. Unfortunately no kills had transpired and despite the fact that the borders frequently pushed out quarry, luck had not been on the small team's side.

But third time out, the gods smiled and the borders, with Rusty in pursuit close behind, shoved out a small vixen. From out of the bracken the fox had bolted across the meadow, heading for a nearby copse. Her judgement of the copse's distance was just out and the collie/greyhound bitch pulled her down, rolling over with the vixen three times before the two came to rest in a heap. By the time the owner of the dogs had got up to them it was all over. The surprising thing was that the Bedlington was hanging on to the fox's throat with a grim deathly grip, refusing to release his hold, even when the other dogs relinquished theirs.

Rusty went on to be a hard dog and he very rarely bolted foxes, but he had his uses when a fox got bottled up in a tight place and was able to rain down blows that caused less game terriers to give up. In such places Rusty as often as not killed his fox in grim deathly silence and to be honest it was stupid to send such a good dog to ground without a locator being used. As a finder and stayer Rusty was quite superb and certainly convinced Jim that the Gutchcommon-bred Bedlington still had the necessary guts and fire to work in a traditional Bedlington manner – bold and quite relentless in the pursuit of his foe.

Lamping
Over a period of time I have met quite a number of individuals who do use Bedlingtons for tasks not normally associated with them. Quite a number of Bedlingtons are used on the lamp and in most cases I know of it has come about quite without planning. A lamper I know had bought a large Bedlington dog pup with the intention

145

of using him as a running dog base line (to cross to greyhounds and whippets) to produce lurchers. Whenever he took his whippet and lurcher out on the dark windy night so beloved of the nocturnal hunters, his Bedlington screamed the place down. The lamper's wife had complained to her husband, 'Either the dog goes lamping with you or you can give up lamping.' 'No contest,' the hunter countered, 'The bugger can come with me.' The next lamping foray came round and with a friend, the two running dogs and the Bedlington, he set forth. Whippets are generally accepted as the fastest running dogs alive over a short sprint, they are also deemed the ones with the least staying power and tire too quickly during the course of a night's lamping. They do, however, recover very rapidly from the early runs, that is to say the first 20 courses of the night (depending on how far the course is and over what terrain). For this reason the whippet bitch in question was always slipped at the first rabbits of the night as the searching beam caught and illuminated their ruby-like eyes. Three rabbits had paid the price of feeding too far out from the sanctuary of the hedgerow's warrens and thrice the squeals of coneys had punctured the black, windy night. On each occasion the Bedlington dog had cart-wheeled round and round trying to slip his collar in order that he might partake in the night-time coursing.

Crossing a ditch into the next field the hunters went, standing with the wind in their faces. They flicked the beam around in the gloom and almost immediately a pair of fox's eyes shone back at them. The collie cross greyhound lurcher bitch flew after the vulpine and bowled the fox just in time for the whippet (also slipped to help the lurcher) to clamp her jaws in a throttling throat-hold worthy of any terrier. 'They've got it,' said the Bedlington's owner, bringing the beam back over the tufts of coarse grass growing in the meadow, 'There's a squatter' (a term used by lampers to describe a rabbit hugging the ground closely to avoid detection). The rabbit was no more than a few yards away from the men and the Bedlington. The Bedlington had seen the coney too and his owner had let go of the baling twine holding him fast through his collar. The Bedlington struck perfectly at his rabbit, picked it up, the rabbit kicked hard and the terrier, keen to stop the struggling, simply bit harder and the struggling stopped.

By now a cold sleet was beginning to fall and the two lampers decided to call it a night and trudge home. As the hunters, now quite cold and wet, approached the last field before the farmhouse, the man operating the lamp flicked on the beam for one last look around. One rabbit was sitting out and both the now tired whippet

A Bedlington and lurcher waiting for a rabbit to bolt.

and collie cross greyhound bolted off after it. After a relatively short course the rabbit was taken and coney number five was in the bag, the whippet returned empty mouthed and the collie cross greyhound bitch retrieved her prize as was so typical of her. 'Good end to the night,' said one of the hunters and both dogs were put on their leads. Just then the Bedlington started pulling hard on his baling twine slip. The lamper flicked on the beam and walking towards them (no doubt attracted by the rabbit's squeal) was a fox. 'Slip the bitch,' said the Bedlington's owner as his friend struggled with rabbits, dead fox and dogs. The man was about to say 'No time', when the Bedlington pulled that little bit harder and slipped free, engaging the fox like a fiend – the dog had taken his second catch of the night.

After this nocturnal jaunt the Bedlington became a regular lamping dog, he was a natural at it and wed to the game with no fuss at all. Whilst it should be pointed out that the dog was never ever light-mouthed (a quality a good lamping dog should possess especially if the rabbits are to be saleable) but he was a demon foxing dog at night, a quarry he would never have worked unless he had been used on the lamp – save for the ones he would encounter in daylight in rough cover. Quite simply, as a terrier the dog was too big, all of 18½ inches, despite the fact that his breeding was all working strain. During the course of his lamping life this outsize Bedlington caught a large number of foxes and accounted for many rabbits and though all of the latter were badly bruised they were appreciated none the less by the lamper's family who did not mind eating a bruised bunny.

From this Bedlington quite a number of good-grade lurchers were bred as all-rounders. His son and daughter (Bedlington cross greyhound hybrids) were quite superb and were a better proposition than their illustrious sire. That is to say, they were better all-rounders, catching rabbits on a run, unlike their sire who could only catch them squatting in a beam. However, their sire's gameness seemed to have been inherited and they made first-class foxing lurchers; perhaps their greatest quality was their common sense, in that they could dish out the necessary measures on a fox, yet be sensible enough to take the rabbits without bruising them.

Mink
You would be quite surprised how many people want a Bedlington to work on mink and quite a lot of questions one gets asked refer to the Bedlington's ability as an aquatic dog. Provided a Bedlington is brought up to accept water as a natural obstruction to be overcome,

just the same as working rough cover for example, then no long-standing problem seems to exist, in fact most Bedlington's seem to like a dip now and again. Further infusions of Glen of Imaal blood will do nothing to deter this, as the latter breed is well known for its love of water.

The continuing rise in the Bedlington's popularity and the increase in mink numbers and its distribution will undoubtedly result in an increase in interest in using the Bedlington (and of course other dogs) on this, the most ferocious of our overseas invaders. I well remember seeing my first mink several years ago while pike fishing. On the opposite bank from which I was angling a large black mink was patrolling so I took note of his whereabouts, thinking I would set a cage for him later. Then there was a swirl in the water in front of me and a hissing sound as nylon fishing line broke the surface following the float and small bream deadbate into the depths below – a swirl quite unlike that of *Esox Lucius*, the great predatory pike. A couple of minutes later would see me net my first zander – another ruthless and unmerciless killer from abroad which, in common with the mink, now ravages our countryside's waterways.

Since that time I have seen countless mink taken by all types of terrier and that of course includes the Bedlington.

Other tasks
As mentioned earlier, sundry tasks often befall the Bedlington. I believe John Piggin tried Floyd of Eakring as a gun dog. Some Bedlingtons become adept at squirrels, but a word of caution – your dog will need to be game and hard mouthed, for a grey squirrel's bite just has to be seen to be believed. I think a game plucky lurcher is better suited for this as squirrels are no slow coaches when running for the trees.

The Bedlington Lurcher

A LTHOUGH THIS IS A book on terriers I felt a brief chapter on the subject of lurchers should be included due to the growing interest in Bedlington cross lurchers. From the number of Bedlington lurchers one sees at the shows and advertised in publications such as *Shooting News* and *Exchange and Mart* one would imagine that many lurcher folk find the Bedlington cross satisfactory in the hunting field. I am fairly sure that most of the Bedlingtons used in these crosses are show-bred dogs. Why then are these dogs so successful as hunters? I believe that the answer to this question is that most greyhound, and working as opposed to show whippets, are game animals and also very sound, it is credit indeed to the enthusiasts of both these breeds that this situation is so today. Hybrid vigour, a strange phenomenon that occurs when two separate breeds are crossed is also likely to play a part.

My preference for breeding a first cross lurcher would be a genuine working strain Bedlington, Rillington or Gutchcommon, alternatively a first or second cross Bedlington-type terrier crossed to a whippet or a good retired racing or coursing greyhound. Progeny bred this way would be ideal ferreting, rough-cover dogs, would lamp well, course hares and stop foxes.

The Bedlington lurcher of old

In the Midlands, lurchers have always been popular, some were called whippets (rather inaccurately) and some were used to compete in the rag racing and Sunday morning rabbit coursing despite their rough wiry coats and obvious terrier influence. Way back in those days between the world wars, many working-class families kept a lurcher and rest assured, reader, such dogs would never be kept if they did not earn their corn. In my own great grandfather's family there were seven boys and two girls plus great grandad and grandmother. Great grandad was a miner, who liked a drink and his dinner on the table when he got home, and ran the household like a dictator – children, wife and the dog had to earn their keep. Let me emphasise the fact that life was hard, money was scarce and 'the old món' as both his sons and daughters called him, expected everything to be done for him, and that included catching as many rabbits as possible to supplement his beer money. This invariably fell on the shoulders of the elder sons and the family pet (though pet seems oddly inaccurate) who was Rose, a rough lurcher bitch, the colour of harvest wheat and with a coat of a linty roughness.

On moonless nights, when the wind ripped wands from the bushes and trees and all was black as coal, Jack and Tom used to venture out with Rose and the long net. By the time the old món got up for his early shift at the pit the rabbits were hanging up gutted, legged and waiting for great grandad to take them to work to sell to his colleagues; that night's beer money was secured, so at least great grandad would be pleased. 'Keep the old món happy and everything will be all right,' would probably have been the family motto, had there been one. While my great grandfather was away working down the mine and the children of school age were at school, the responsibility of feeding the bantams and the pig and seeing to and handling the ferrets fell on my great grandmother's shoulders along with doing all the wifely chores which were not just expected of her but were demanded, no less. If great grandad were around nowadays, doubtless he would have been a candidate for the divorce courts.

Even the responsibility of looking after Rose the rough wheaton-coloured lurcher bitch was great grandma's, and on certain days instructions were left that while the lord and master was away at the pit, some wealthy businessmen from the now well-to-do and expanding industrial city of Birmingham would be calling to borrow Rose for a day's rabbiting. The rewards for such a loan were a couple of pounds in money and often as not a joint of meat as well, and any surplus rabbits went to supplement great grandad's beer money fund. Such was Rose's reputation that loaning the bitch became a regular occurrence. Many years after, I enquired as to the breeding of the now long dead Rose; my own grandfather told me Rose was a cross between a Bedlington and a small whippet cross greyhound.

Bedlington crosses and collie crosses were the traditional ways of

A Bedlington/whippet cross Bedlington/greyhound (left) and a Bedlington/greyhound (right).

A first cross Bedlington/whippet.

producing a lurcher in the industrial Midlands, and even today those crosses are still the most favoured. Bedlington cross whippet lurchers, especially the genuine first cross are very popular the country over, the type of animal Jack Hargreaves referred to in his Channel 4 TV programme *Old Country* as 'the coney dog' that did the job of long stop when ferreting – that is to say if a rabbit threw the purse net as it bolted, the rabbiting dog was expected to nail it on the run. Old Rose did this all those years ago, and on occasions, especially if plenty of rabbits had already been caught, great grandad would leave a purse net off a hole on purpose, point to Rose and say, 'that one's yours.' Needless to say Rose was expected to catch the coney if one obliged and bolted.

The Bedlington/greyhound lurcher
The Bedlington/greyhound cross can do everything you are likely to require from a lurcher and I would not hesitate to course one on either a hare or a fox; believe me, one of these crosses can stop either. Levelling out at approximately 22 to 26 inches, black/blue or red/fawn and rough coated, the Bedlington/greyhound combines the best of both worlds, greyhound speed and terrier grit. Three-quarter sighthound, quarter Bedlington crosses are also very popular and here again I favour the greyhound version of the three-quarter bred; the Bedlington guts and drive is still fairly apparent though one should not forget most greyhounds are also extremely gutsy animals, as a glance at many racing greyhounds will prove, especially when they look at animals, even slightly smaller than themselves, a little unhealthily.

Another variation on the three-quarter sighthound cross were two dogs owned by Fred Newman – a working saluki dog had been paired to a first cross Bedlington/greyhound bitch. The two examples Fred had were quite biddable and were probably among some of the best lampers I have ever seen. At fox they were fearless, not holding back at all and inclined to be mixers. At one time quite a number of lurchers from this type of breeding were being produced in the Leicester area.

A gentleman from Birmingham who has a 15 inch blue Bedlington bitch called Lassie works her under factories and uses a Bedlington/greyhound lurcher bitch and an American pit bull terrier/greyhound dog hybrid to run down the foxes she frequently bolts. Where applicable Harry nets his foxes and frees them where they will cause no further harm, but often he gets called to move them from where netting is not possible and it is here that his lurchers come into play. In one hunt, Harry was at an engineering factory site, where foxes had made an earth under one wall of the factory (in a vent) and, crossing the factory football pitch, were taking all manner of delicacies from the contents of dustbins to fancy poultry, pet rabbits and meat waste from a butchers waiting to go to a local maggot farm.

Harry's reputation as a fox-man was well known by the local community and after cowboy lampers had been caught frequently trying to course the foxes at night with highly unsuitable dogs, Harry had been asked by the factory owner to deal with them. With nowhere to place nets properly Harry was faced with the decision to course the foxes if he could persuade them to bolt. Harry looked around. 'Two ways for them to bolt,' he had told the factory owner, 'Up there,' pointing to a disused railway embankment, 'or across the soccer pitch.' Positioning the Bedlington/greyhound at the railings by the embankment he placed his bull terrier/greyhound dog in a position to stop anything from crossing the soccer pitch.

Harry had sighed and gone with Lassie the Bedlington bitch to the vent. 'You do know if she gets stuck that factory floor's gonna come up, don't you?' he had said to the factory owner and though the latter might have thought Harry was joking, he would have been wrong and most certainly it would not have been the first time a factory floor had come up to liberate Lassie with an awkward fox bottled up. Lassie was then entered and barely a minute had gone by when a vixen flashed out going hell for leather towards the embankment. She went between two cars and the Bedlington/ greyhound caught her as she came out the other side. 'Jesus Christ,' the factory owner whistled as the lurcher shook the fox, 'That were bloody fast.'

Barely had the owner had a chance to recover, when another fox streaked out of the vent closely followed by Lassie who was screaming like a Banshee. The bull/greyhound closed in to take the fox, which quite suddenly jinked away from the football pitch and the thundering power-house of bull/greyhound heading its way and bolted through the open factory doors followed by Lassie and the two lurchers. Apparently all four had thundered along the factory gangway, narrowly missing a fork-lift truck carrying stillages of foundry castings. However, by now the lurchers had overtaken Lassie and the bull/greyhound caught the fox as it turned by some machinery. By the time Harry and the factory owner reached them, all three dogs were pulling the dead fox out of the suds tank of a large capstan lathe.

All three dogs were spattered in oil, suds and swarf (metal cuttings). 'That little dog of yours is a good 'un mate,' a machine operator had said to Harry, 'but it looks like a bloody lamb. What breed is it?' Harry put his hands on his knees, looked at the operator and wheezed, 'a Bedlington terrier.' 'It's a bleedin' good 'un, pal,' the impressed operator continued, 'A bleedin' good 'un.'

Bedlington/whippet lurcher
In Wales, Bedlington/whippet first crosses are very much in vogue, where it is often as not regarded as the best cross for purpose-bred rabbiting dogs. I have worked both pure bred whippets and Bedlingtons, and tend to think the whippet is a better proposition at the rabbit-catching game than the hybrid. The only advantage the hybrid holds in my opinion, is the fact you get a better coat and skin than a whippet's. I do know quite a number of Bedlington/ whippets who are reputed as being good little workers and their owners swear by them. On looks I like the Bedlington/whippet I must confess, and while they may not be the all-round lurcher the Bedlington/greyhound is, they can indeed make superb rabbiting dogs.

The Bedlington cross greyhound/whippet lurcher
The hybrid Bedlington/greyhound/whippet comes very much uniform in type, all are rough coated and black/blue or fawn. From time to time one sees adverts for smooth-coated and brindled coloured examples reputedly bred this way; personally I would be very suspicious of any dog carrying these characteristics certainly as a first cross. What I do suggest is they are second crosses back either to a whippet or a greyhound, or possibly pedigree-unknown lurchers.

Bedlington/lakeland cross whippet lurcher
Norman, George Newcombe's first cross Bedlington/lakeland hybrid served many bitches ranging from working and show-type Bedlingtons to certain running dogs. Rather contradicting what I have just said, Norman did produce in a mating with a whippet bitch one brindled pup, whether the lakeland breeding had something to do with this is of course purely guesswork. One of Norman's pups, a bitch, blue and tan in colour, out of John Piggin's Lena, was acquired by Les Robinson of South Humberside; Amy, as Les called the bitch, grew to be a very big terrier, 19 inches in fact. An ardent fan of Bedlington-blooded lurchers Les envisaged her as a good base for producing his ideal lurcher, suited to the type of terrain he hunted. When at last he bred from Amy he used Cowdells Will Hay, a dog that had quite a reputation as a speed

A three-quarter Bedlington/quarter whippet.

A fine Bedlington lurcher.

merchant as his race times proved. From the Amy/Will Hay pairing, Les obtained, according to reports, a better version of the Bedlington/whippet type cross, his pups were half greyhound, eighth lakeland, three-eights Bedlington and were still a Bedlington-type lurcher in their appearance; the Bedlington dominance always seems to show through even in quarter and eighth Bedlington crosses.

Many of the whippet lurchers that were used for rag racing and organised rabbit coursing were bred this way, (three-quarter whippet/quarter Bedlington), especially in Yorkshire and the Midlands.

The Bedlington/collie/greyhound lurcher

My other favourite version of the Bedlington lurcher just has to be stated at this point and it combines both Bedlington and collie genes and before the reader starts thinking a slap-dash lurcher was flung together, let me stress this breeding programme was very scientifically thought out. The very best Bedlington type lurchers it has ever been my privilege to meet were bred in the way I am about to describe.

A yellow-eyed red collie (some would call it liver) was paired to a greyhound bitch, this first cross was in turn mated to a greyhound dog; a bitch called Fly from the mating (a liver/red lurcher) was paired to a well-known Bedlington/greyhound dog; the resulting litter included a blue/black bitch, which was an excellent example of Bedlington/collie and greyhound blood judiciously blended together. The person who eventually acquired Blue lamped her at rabbits, hares and fox, well known now for his Irish-bred Glen of Imaal terriers, this owner decided to breed a litter with Blue after she broke a wrist chasing a cat up a lamp post and landed awkwardly.

Blue was paired to Dick, a black greyhound dog barred from a local flapping track for turning his head and fighting. He was of unknown quality, as no written details of his breeding were available, though he had been coursed at hare and fox. Dick took great delight at the latter, killing swiftly and with no mess.

Dick, so super fit, stormed up to hares with comparative ease but, like many speed merchants, never found hares easy; their twisting turns made him regularly overshoot and gave puss its vital yards to make good its escape. Dick's owner laid the dog up to let his muscles become slightly less hardened and stiff. Dick used his new-found elasticity to good effect, and anyone who doubts this would do well to talk to racing greyhound trainers who state that super-fit greyhounds are prone to muscle strains and sprains.

Dick, when paired to Blue, the Bedlington-type lurcher sired an initial litter of 10 pups, both rough-coated Bedlington types (though they were in actual fact only one-eighth Bedlington) and smooth-coated greyhound types. John Varley of Stoke Golding obtained the black bitch called Sobers (after Gary Sobers the cricketer). Sobers' reputation as an all-rounder is well known; not only did she make an efficient rabbit bitch, she coursed hare with success and is absolutely deadly on fox. John's brother Mick Varley, well-known for his smooth-coated black fell terrier bitch Ranter obtained Jet. (I had seen Jet course hare before Varley obtained her and knew of her prowess in the hunting field.)

Considering Mick was better known as a supporter of working-dog shows, he worked Jet regularly enough, and the last time I saw her prior to her untimely death, she was covered in scars, some were obviously from barbed wire, others were decidely vulpine in appearance. Jet's career was cut short by a collision with a telegraph pole, while chasing a rabbit running away in a beam, producing a severe shoulder injury which caused the leg to wither, and despite veterinary help, Jet had to be put to sleep. A sad end for a valiant dog, made even sadder by the fact that I do not think Jet had yet peaked nor had she bred any pups.

Of the Bedlington-type lurchers produced by Blue none was better known than Bill Greenway's Spring. If ever a dog was going to be used on the lamp it was Spring; his reputation as a worker is well known, as is his standing as a stud dog. People tend to refer to Spring as a Bedlington/greyhound, showing how dominant are Bedlington genes, even in eighth-bred specimens. Blue, the mother of them all, has a place, and a very special one at that in my heart, for no dog ever taught me more about the ways of hunting than this bitch, even though I had been brought up with whippets, greyhounds and Russell-type terriers. When Fred offered her to me I jumped at the chance, and with Blue, I lamped rabbits, caught them in daylight, coursed hares and foxes, and even used her at rats.

When Blue came into season again I was eager to breed a litter from her and chose a lurcher rather than a pure sighthound this time – a blue and white marked collie/whippet cross collie/greyhound. From this pairing came a quite famous lurcher show-winner, Jimmy, a smooth black dog which John Varley had and which eventually he paired to the hard-nut Sobers. A real eye-catching liver/red collie type of lurcher was the end result, as

Sobers a hard type of foxing lurcher.

Will one bolt?

opposed to a Bedlington or greyhoundy type dog, a result of the two red-collie genes coming together from both Sobers and Jimmy. The specimen I saw was a perfect liver lurcher with the hazel eyes, light-brown nose and red nails, colours any owner of a liver-coloured Bedlington terrier would have been proud of.

Now Blue is an old retired veteran who sleeps in the house and has a slight heart condition, but less than 12 months from the time of writing she was still catching rabbits by her own choice, perhaps not coursing them but taking them like she always had done, in hedgerows and as they bolted from cover (I have always been amazed how easily she did this) or alternatively taking a squatter.

My old Blue taught me a lot of the ways of rabbits and I dedicate this chapter of my book to Blue. Thank you, my old friend, I shall always be in your debt, for you showed me the way of the true working dog, brave, courageous, loyal, and always in the right place at the right time.

So many people criticise the Bedlington lurchers for being hard mouthed on a rabbit, or at least claim they are. I do not believe this to be a very valid criticism as most Beddies are intelligent enough to hold lightly a rabbit or hare and to dish out the necessary measures on a fox (as do many lurcher types irrespective of their relevant breeding). My recommendation is this, if you do get a Bedlington lurcher, I do not think you will be disappointed, and if you get one that gives you as much pleasure as old Blue did me, consider yourself a lucky person.

Just after this book was completed, old Blue passed peacefully away.

Blue, a much missed friend.